## Welcome to the Upside Down

**T**aking the world by storm when it first dropped in 2016, *Stranger Things* combined all the best bits of sci-fi, horror and '80s nostalgia to create a world that had viewers gripped from the very start. In this bookazine, we take you on an epic journey to Hawkins, Indiana, to explore the roots of Netflix's smash-hit show and to celebrate its monster success. You'll find profiles of the series' much-loved – and some less so – characters, meet the horrifying creatures of the Upside Down and discover in-depth, episode-by-episode breakdowns of the four seasons so far.

And that's not all! For all the superfans out there, we've also got a host of awesome free gifts – a huge double-sided A1 poster, three frameable art cards and four premium postcards, all featuring a selection of memorable moments from the series and some of your best-loved characters.

So what are you waiting for?

# Eerie Indiana

## HOW A PAIR OF BROTHERS BLENDED SECRET CIA EXPERIMENTS, A CAST OF RELATIVE UNKNOWNS AND A LOVE OF '80S MOVIES TO MAKE A SMASH-HIT TV SHOW

WORDS **RICHARD EDWARDS**

The Duffer brothers weren't old enough to watch the movies that inspired their hit Netflix series, *Stranger Things*, when they were released in cinemas. But despite being born in 1984 – the year *after* the show's first season is set – Matt and Ross's childhoods were shaped by the pop culture of a decade they're too young to remember. Growing up in North Carolina, the twins spent their childhoods playing Dungeons & Dragons, and devouring VHS tapes of classics like *The Goonies* and *ET* "on rotation" – enough to form a cinematic memory of an era when the effects-driven blockbuster really came into its own.

"I think when you're first watching and discovering movies, at that magic age of eight to 12, they're very powerful," Matt pointed out before *Stranger Things'* first season aired. "Those movies had a huge impact on a lot of us. It's a world we know and understand – we grew up there."

While the Duffers' affection for '80s movies was far from extraordinary, few choose to channel that passion into a TV series – and even fewer persuade a broadcaster or streaming service to join them on the ride. But Netflix saw the potential in the brothers' tale of, well, strange things going on in a small Indiana town, and gave the show the cherished green light.

Ahead of its 2016 launch, however, there was little to suggest it was about to become one of the most popular TV shows on the planet. The likes of *House of Cards, Orange is the New Black* and *Daredevil* had made the industry (and awards ceremonies) take notice of the upstart streaming service, but with *The Crown, The Witcher* and *Bridgerton* still to come, Netflix was still looking for a blockbuster smash of *Game of Thrones* proportions. And in an era when recognisable franchises had come to dominate, few would have tipped this unfamiliar story – whose biggest star, Winona Ryder, was no longer a Hollywood A-lister – to capture the zeitgeist.

The eight episodes of season one dropped simultaneously on 15 July 2016, and something magical happened. *Stranger Things* was suddenly the show that *everybody* was talking about – following the death of a supporting character, "Justice for Barb" even became a popular rallying cry online – and the million-dollar question was less about whether you'd watched it, than how quickly you'd binged the whole lot. And while Netflix was traditionally cagey about its viewing figures, there was never any doubt that the Duffers' ode to the '80s had become a blockbuster as big as any of the movies that inspired it.

"I knew it was good, but we had no idea whether people would tune in," producer Shawn Levy said in 2017.

"I remember as early as the day after launch, the volume of social media I started seeing was astonishing. Within a week it felt like a wave, and within a month it felt like a tsunami."

"We were just trying to tell a story that we knew we would want to watch," Ross Duffer recalled. "We thought that it would appeal to people like us who were nostalgic for this type of storytelling, but I guess what surprised us the most was that it reached a much broader audience than that. For younger people who aren't necessarily as nostalgic for this type of thing to embrace it like they have was a great surprise."

## AMBLIN ALONG

Before *Stranger Things*, little on the Duffers' CV hinted at

what was to come. They'd written and directed a little-seen 2015 post-apocalyptic movie called *Hidden* and scripted three episodes of M Night Shyamalan's own tale of a spooky town, *Wayward Pines*, but they were light years from the A-list until their pilot script attracted Shawn Levy's attention.

Levy was well established in Hollywood thanks to his popular *Night at the Museum* movies – he's since directed *Free Guy* and Netflix's own *The Adam Project* – and, unlike the Duffers, was old enough to remember the '80s the first time around. He saw something special in the story, and would become the third corner of the show's core creative triumvirate.

"I was immediately struck by how propulsively it was paced," he recalled back in 2017. "I think that's an interesting

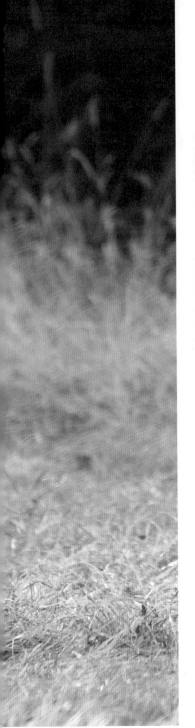

**Above:** The Duffer hive mind in action – Ross and Matt call the shots on *Stranger Things'* first season.

**Left:** David Harbour was arguably best known for a bit part in *Quantum of Solace* before playing Hawkins' beloved police chief Jim Hopper.

first impression, given how bingeable it later became. And in spite of its hooky mystery and period setting, it carved really three-dimensional and complex characters, where so many period shows and movies have that kitschy hook without servicing character."

Despite becoming best known for its nostalgia, *Stranger Things* didn't start out as a celebration of the movies of the Duffers' youth. Instead, the twins were looking to tell a story based on the infamous real-life MKUltra programme, where the CIA performed covert experiments in mind control from the 1950s through to the '70s. The influence is clear in the show's Hawkins National Laboratory, where shady scientists use a young girl with telekinetic powers as a test subject, and inadvertently open a door to a frightening parallel world known as the Upside Down.

"Honestly, what started this was us remembering the time when we believed that the government was doing these shady experiments," Ross Duffer said in 2017. "We were looking at *Altered States* and films like that, and thinking we wanted to go back to that Cold War paranoia. That's originally how the conversation started, and it's what led back to these '80s movies that we fell in love with. It started with this idea [of] whether we believed that events like this could be possible somewhere like small-town America. Then that led us to thinking, 'This is when all of our favourite movies are set!' and all those ideas merged together."

While the Duffers hadn't experienced the '80s first hand, they did have an instinctive feel for what made the movies of the era tick. Primarily influenced by Steven Spielberg and his Amblin Entertainment production company – the outfit behind the suburban family-friendly thrills of *Poltergeist*, *Gremlins*, *The Goonies* and *Back to the Future* – they identified a common "sense of wonder and awe in a setting that is very relatable." The similarities are clear in *Stranger Things*, where a quartet of ordinary pre-teens find themselves experiencing close encounters of the supernatural kind, after one of their number – Will Byers – is pulled into the Upside Down.

"We started looking at these films and thinking what it was about them that made us love them so much," Matt said in 2016. "For us it was the juxtaposition of the ordinary and

**Above:** *Stranger Things* gave Winona
Ryder her best role in years, as a mother
desperately searching for her son, Will.

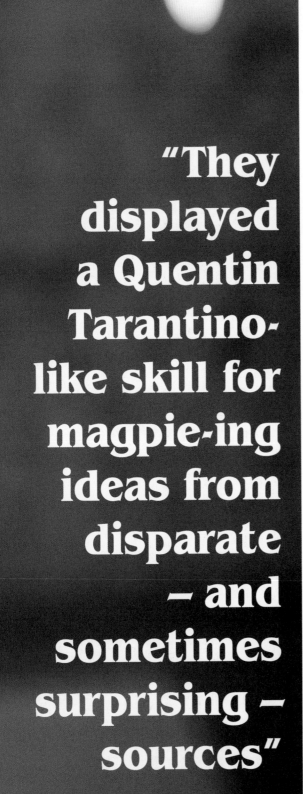

"They displayed a Quentin Tarantino-like skill for magpie-ing ideas from disparate – and sometimes surprising – sources"

the extraordinary. We had very ordinary suburban lives, and these films tapped into that. They made us think, 'Oh my God, maybe I'm going to find a treasure map in the attic,' or 'What if we find an alien out in the woods?'"

But the Duffers did something more than simply create a televisual cover version of Amblin's greatest hits. Instead, they displayed a Quentin Tarantino-like skill for magpie-ing ideas from disparate – and sometimes surprising – sources. Will's disappearance, for example, has echoes of the abduction of Laura Palmer in David Lynch's *Twin Peaks*, while the twins found inspiration in darker, more grown-up fare from the back catalogues of Stephen King and body horror pioneer David Cronenberg. The fingerprints of John Carpenter, director of *Halloween* and *The Thing*, are also visible throughout – not least in the show's evocative synth score by Kyle Dixon and Michael Stein.

"When we were first pitching the series around we made a demo reel where we took all these different movies that have inspired us – the Carpenter stuff, the Spielberg stuff – and we scored it with John Carpenter music," Ross Duffer revealed in 2016. "When we put the theme music over *ET*, not only did we realise that it worked but it gave it this exciting edge."

## ONCE YOU POP, YOU CAN'T STOP

In hindsight, tapping a wave of nostalgia as *Stranger Things* did seems something of a no-brainer. The show landed on Netflix within a year of the unashamedly retro *The Force Awakens* – a film precision engineered to remind *Star Wars* fans why they fell in love with the saga in the first place – and over the last year, *Ghostbusters: Afterlife*, *The Matrix Resurrections* and *Spider-Man: No Way Home* have all been built around audiences' love of revisiting the past.

But there was more to *Stranger Things'* success than timing. Indeed, future *The Force Awakens* director JJ Abrams had ventured into similar territory in 2011 with *Super 8*, but his own love letter to Spielberg – about a bunch of kids whose efforts to make a movie unwittingly record an alien escaping a train crash – was a more modest hit. It also lacked the multi-generational appeal that *Stranger Things* has in abundance, an ability to draw in a generation for whom phones with wires come from a world even more alien than the Upside Down.

"The [best '80s films] don't feel '80s, they feel timeless," Matt Duffer said of the show's era in 2016. "You show a kid one now and nothing feels '80s about it. That was something we were conscious of. It was important that nothing felt too kitschy. Sure, there's a Millennium Falcon toy there and an *Evil Dead* poster here, but it would have been the same style and music if we were shooting a show in 2016."

The Duffers also displayed a very modern instinct for storytelling, exploiting Netflix's all-in-one-go release strategy with cliffhangers that made you desperate to binge the next episode straight away – the televisual equivalent of Pringles' "once you pop, you can't stop" slogan.

"I guess we wrote it and tried to structure it as much as possible like a big eight-hour movie," Matt Duffer admitted ahead of season two. "The cool thing about Netflix is you could spread it out and do one episode a week – though I think we try to make it as hard as possible for you to do that, as we tend to end on these cliffhangers.

"That kind of came about by accident. We always liked having a little teaser leading into the main titles, because we always wanted the opening of the episode to give you a little bit of a rush, and in order to do that it ended up that we would cut out the climax from the episode before and put it into the beginning of the next episode. It was not designed to drive binge-viewing, but I think that it did end up doing that!"

## THESE GO TO ELEVEN

Look past the nostalgia, the cliffhangers and the freaky parallel world, however, and arguably the biggest reason for *Stranger Things*' phenomenal success is its characters and the actors who play them – after all, unleashing Demogorgons on an unsuspecting small town counts for nothing if you don't care about the people in harm's way.

It's perhaps appropriate that a show so steeped in Amblin lore should have displayed such a Spielbergian knack for picking child actors, and the four boys at the centre of the story – Mike (Finn Wolfhard), Lucas (Caleb McLaughlin), Dustin (Gaten Matarazzo) and Will (Noah Schnapp) – were all natural successors to the Goonies. Perhaps the most important find, though, was Millie Bobby Brown, the young British actor who became the face of the show playing Eleven, the little girl with close-cropped hair whose telekinetic abilities result in characteristic nosebleeds.

But *Stranger Things* was never just about the kids. From the beginning, it seamlessly blended parallel storylines about the teens and the grown-ups caught up in Will's disappearance, providing entry points for every generation clicking through Netflix's navigation screen. So where younger viewers were more likely to get caught up in Mike, Lucas and Dustin's adventures on their improbable, parent-defying quest to rescue their best friend, adults could relate to Joyce's (Winona Ryder)'s palpable grief at the loss of her son – and her belief that she can communicate with him through the walls of her house, even though everyone in the town thinks she's mad.

Along with fellow '80s/'90s veteran Matthew Modine (who played morally dubious laboratory scientist Dr

**Below:** The gang of misfits are joined by new fans' favourite Eddie Munson (centre) in season four.

**Below:** She only appeared in a couple of episodes, but Shannon Purser's Barb became the focus of an unlikely fan movement.

**Below:** The kids look for a portal to the Upside Down.

Martin Brenner), Ryder was by some distance the biggest name in a show that was – initially, at least – seriously short on star power.

Of course, that all changed when the show hit the stratosphere, as the stars became seriously hot property in Hollywood, and big enough to headline blockbuster movies: most notably, Millie Bobby Brown has topped the bill in *Godzilla: King of the Monsters* and *Enola Holmes*, David Harbour (police chief Hopper) has starred in *Hellboy* and *Black Widow*, and Finn Wolfhard has taken major roles in the *IT* movies and *Ghostbusters: Afterlife*. Even nominal supporting players like Joe Keery – whose elegantly coiffed Steve Harrington has evolved from school bully to comedic powerhouse – are bankable enough to take major roles in the likes of *Free Guy*.

## SEQUEL OPPORTUNITIES

Where success leads, sequels tend to follow, and a Halloween-set second season – inventively titled *Stranger Things 2* – arrived little over a year after its predecessor. In the tradition of James Cameron classics *Aliens* and *Terminator 2*, the Duffers upped the ante by expanding

the scope and introducing a bigger threat – in this case the colossal Mind Flayer. But they also played around with the formula, to embrace the fact that their young cast were getting older – by the time the third season arrived in 2019, John Hughes high school movies were just as big an inspiration as all those Amblin classics.

"You have to take [the kids ageing] into account in the narrative," Matt Duffer said ahead of season two. "It's funny, though, that in the story they were normal kids in season one and then they go through this extraordinary thing that's changed them. In a way that's also happened in their real lives, because they were very real kids last year and they went through an extraordinary change when the show came out. Now they're these little celebrities."

With the world having returned to Hawkins in May 2022 for season four, it seems the show is growing up once again. Even three years after our last visit, Eleven, Hopper, Joyce, Mike and the rest are characters you still want to hang out with, with that small Indiana town remaining one of the hottest destinations on TV. Not bad for a story born from two brothers' love of VHS tapes from the now-distant past.

# The Characters

# THE MYSTERIOUS GIRL AT THE SHOW'S CENTRE, ELEVEN HAS BEEN THROUGH MORE IN HER SHORT TIME THAN MOST GO THROUGH IN A LIFETIME

WORDS **STEVE WRIGHT**

The closest thing that Stranger Things has to a protagonist, Eleven (Millie Bobby Brown) – has, more than any other character in the show, been through the mill.

Taken from her mother as a child, El was denied all the things children usually take for granted: care, a family, friends – even a name. Her only moniker comes from the number she has tattooed on her arm.

But that's not the worst of it. Frequently experimented on and punished by the sinister Dr Brenner, her accidental opening of the gate to the Upside Down at Hawkins Lab provides El with the means to escape. This leads to her first encounter with friendly normality in the form of Mike, Dustin and Lucas.

While helping look for their missing friend, Will Byers, she experiences some of the things she was missing: friendship, school, Eggo waffles – even love, as hers and Mike's bond proves to be a strong one. Plus, she makes a bully wet himself. Can't say fairer than that.

Using her powers, she helps rescue Will and destroy the Demogorgon, seemingly sacrificing herself in the process. In reality, she has been transported to the Upside Down, which she quickly escapes from. Eventually being taken in by Hopper, the two form a paternal bond of sorts, although she eventually grows frustrated with his protective nature.

After a road trip to Chicago – encountering her lobotomised mother on the way – she returns to Hawkins, helping to save the day once more, this time from the Mind Flayer, as she's reunited with Mike and the gang.

From here, things take a brighter turn as Hopper ensures her future by having her legally adopted as his daughter, Jane Hopper. As a further sweetener, she gets to attend the Snow Ball with Mike, where the two share a kiss.

From there, El begins the transition into a typical teenager – dating Mike, hanging out with her new friend Max, and giving her dad all manner of worries.

It's not long before the Upside Down resurfaces as a threat once more, however, with even El struggling against the Mind Flayer-possessed Billy Hargrove.

In spite of this, El is still able to help save the day – although tragically, Hopper seemingly dies in the process. Devastated, El is taken in by Joyce Byers, and the two leave for California alongside Jonathan and Will.

Maintaining a facade that everything's okay, El struggles in California. Bullied for her naive and innocent nature, and worried about Mike's physical and metaphorical distance, she jumps at the chance to regain her powers.

Meeting up with Brenner and Owens once more, we discover the truth behind the threat of the Upside Down: she inadvertently helped make it one. Having banished a young Henry Creel – before he became Vecna – there, it seems that Brenner's influence was even more nefarious than we originally thought.

Newly repowered, she is able to fight off Vecna, although too late to stop him putting Max in a coma. Back in Hawkins with her friends – including Mike – she's going to need to be on top form when Vecna returns.

## ELEVEN

## LIVING PROOF THAT AN IN-DEPTH KNOWLEDGE OF DUNGEONS & DRAGONS CAN SAVE LIVES

WORDS **STEVE WRIGHT**

If there's a character that goes under the radar in Stranger Things, it's Mike Wheeler (Finn Wolfhard). While everyone hails Eleven, Hopper, Dustin and Steve Harrington, Mike's at the centre of it all, quietly holding everything together.

Really, it's almost his story. It's his best friend who goes missing, and it's he who shelters Eleven when she first shows up. It's almost like Elliott meeting ET, except right from the off it's clear that Mike has feelings for her.

While Mike, Dustin, Lucas and Will have each other, they are nonetheless bullied outsiders. For this reason, Mike immediately empathises with El, and goes to great lengths to keep her safe.

This loyalty continues to show itself in season two: refusing to believe El is dead, he calls her every night using his Supercom,

and shows concern for Will when it becomes clear his friend's stay in the Upside Down has left a mark.

Still, as always, everything comes back to Dungeons & Dragons. Mike is a born dungeon master, and it's his and his friends' realisation of the Upside Down's monster's similarity to the game's Mind Flayer that informs their tactics on how to stop it.

Best of all, El returns to help save the day, leading to an emotional reunion with Mike. The day saved, there's even time for them to share a tender moment during their first dance at the Snow Ball.

The following year, the two are fully in the throes of teenage passion – despite the increasingly futile attempts of El's new guardian, Hopper, to get between them. Sure, there are hitches – they briefly break up after Hopper tells Mike to stay away from her, after which El uses her power to spy on Mike – but it's fairly standard for young love.

Regardless, soon enough the Mind Flayer is back, and it's Mike's turn to save El for a change, clubbing a possessed Billy with a baseball bat in the process, before witnessing the big confrontation that sees the Mind Flayer apparently destroyed once and for all.

However, the ending is bittersweet. With Hopper apparently dead, El is forced to leave Hawkins with the Byers family. It may be goodbye, but not forever, as they promise to see each other soon.

As it turns out, five months is a long time. While Mike has made new friends in the Hellfire Club, those closest to him are struggling big time: El is being bullied, and Will feels distant from his best friend. When he goes to visit for spring break, matters come to a head, and things look even worse for them.

Still, Mike and Will pull themselves together in time to formulate a plan to rescue El, and help her into the Upside Down to take on Vecna. While the encounter doesn't go entirely to plan, the season closes on a note of hope, with Mike and El back together, and in Hawkins together with their closest friends.

# Dustin Henderson

## THE BEATING HEART OF THE GROUP IS UTTERLY LOVEABLE IN EVERY WAY

WORDS **STEVE WRIGHT**

The beating heart and gentle soul of the group, Dustin (Gaten Matarazzo) is many people's favourite character, and for good reason. He's a peacemaker, full of determination, and brings out the best in people.

Like his best friends, Mike Wheeler, Lucas Sinclair and Will Byers, Dustin is a Dungeons & Dragons devotee and committed member of the school's AV club. It's these interests that come to the fore when Will goes missing.

Throughout the saga of Will's disappearance and the subsequent arrival into their lives of Eleven, Dustin plays a proactive role, getting vital information from their teacher, Mr Clarke, and making sure that Mike and Lucas reconcile after El saves them from some bullies. During this first season, he proves to be the glue in the group, keeping them on track right until Will is rescued.

The following year, Dustin has two things on his mind: games and girls. More specifically, who keeps beating their high scores at Palace Arcade? New arrival Max Mayfield proves to be the answer to both questions.

While he initially battles Lucas for her affections, his true love this season is Dart, a miniature Demogorgon he unwittingly befriends. Turns out he'll forgive him anything, even eating the family cat, Mews.

A slightly more fruitful relationship is the one he develops with a certain Steve Harrington. Having enlisted Steve's help against the Demogorgons, Steve becomes something of a father figure to Dustin, something he's clearly missing. Steve offers advice on girls, the secret of

how to have incredible hair, and even drops him off outside the Snow Ball.

While the end-of-year finale is unsuccessful on the girlfriend front for Dustin, his spirits are lifted by Nancy Wheeler, who cheers him up by offering him the slow dance his peers had denied him, in one of the show's most heartwarming moments.

As it turns out, Dustin doesn't have to wait too long for some romance, meeting a girl named Suzie at Camp Know Where, with Dustin even building a ham radio device (named 'Cerebro', naturally) in order to make sure the two stay in touch.

Not that any of his friends really believe him – indeed, it's a strange time for Dustin. With Mike and Lucas paired up with El and Max, Dustin ends up spending most of his time with Steve and Robin at the Starcourt Mall when he unintentionally manages to intercept a Russian transmission on Cerebro.

After discovering another gate below the mall, he and his friends once again team up to defeat the Mind Flayer – his and Suzie's rendition of 'Neverending Story' over Cerebro providing the utterly awesome centrepiece.

The following summer, he is again the good guy of the group, vouching for Eddie's innocence and helping come up with the plan for combating Vecna.

Unfortunately, it's not to be a happy ending this time, with Eddie dying in Dustin's arms, but not before making him promise to look after Hawkins' fellow misfits. He may have faced real tragedy for the first time, but we know he won't let anyone down.

# Lucas Sinclair

## AS THE DUNGEON AND WEAPONS MASTER, LUCAS IS THE LEVEL-HEADED TACTICIAN OF THE GROUP

WORDS **STEVE WRIGHT**

A core member of the gang at the heart of Stranger Things, Lucas (Caleb McLaughlin) is best friends with Will Byers, Dustin Henderson and Mike Wheeler, sharing a love of all things geeky, especially Dungeons & Dragons.

When Will goes missing and the group first encounter Eleven, we get a bit more of an idea of the dynamic of the group: while Mike and Dustin are more believing of her, Lucas is the sceptic. This outlook isn't helped when it turns out that El is deliberately keeping them from the Upside Down (understandably, in fairness), but Lucas isn't happy. He's even less happy when she telekinetically hurls him after he gets in a fight with Mike.

Still, as tends to happen after kids fight, they quickly make up, but not before Lucas successfully warns the gang of trouble afoot. Later on, he joins the group as they help El defeat the Demogorgon before reuniting with the rescued Will.

A year later, and it's love in the air as redhead Max Mayfield arrives on the scene. Unfortunately, she also has an absolutely terrifying older step-brother, Billy, who isn't averse to casually trying to run Lucas and co off the road.

Regardless, this doesn't put Lucas or Dustin off vying for Max's affections, accepting her into the group even while they have bigger fish to fry, what with looking after mini Demogorgon 'Dart'.

Ultimately, it's Lucas who wins this particular battle, kissing Max at the Snow Ball in the season two finale. A

year later, and they're still together, bickering like a regular married couple beyond their tender years and, more often than not, hanging out at Starcourt Mall.

In the group, Lucas seems to take on the role of an elder statesman of sorts, dishing out relationship advice to a grateful Mike (even though it's not always good advice), and helping out as Hawkins comes under assault yet again from the fearsome creatures that inhabit the Upside Down.

Yet he's far more than just the level-headed one; he's a born tactician and natural leader, helming the boys' Dungeons & Dragons sessions, adept at using a slingshot, and not afraid to stand up to bullies – or in the case of Billy, absolutely terrifying older brothers.

He also shows real signs of coming of age, accepting El into the group, later forgiving her for spying on him and Mike, asking for advice when it's needed (like when he asked his dad about how to apologise to girls), and gifting their beloved D&D set to his irritating younger sister Erica.

Now in high school, Lucas starts to drift from the group, – and (although not by his choice) Max, forgoing D&D in favour of the school basketball team. He's back with his friends before long though, helping Max through her first encounter with Vecna (assisted by Kate Bush, of course).

However, when he has to fight off deranged jock Jason Carver, he can only watch helplessly as Max is brutally attacked and killed, only for Eleven to bring her back. Dutifully staying by her bedside, we truly hope they'll get the chance to have that date.

# Will Byers

## THIS POOR BOY HAS ENDURED MORE THAN PEOPLE TRIPLE HIS AGE, BUT HIS ROCK-SOLID RESOLVE NEVER WAVERS

WORDS **DREW SLEEP**

A quiet kid living in the tranquil woodland outskirts of Hawkins, the life of Will Byers (Noah Schnapp) turned quite literally upside down when he was abducted by an otherworldly creature on 6 November 1983. Before the ordeal, Will was a sweet lad who enjoyed playing Dungeons & Dragons with his friends Mike, Dustin and Lucas, and enjoyed the company of his mother Joyce and older brother Jonathan. He was well-liked by those he loved, and for a good reason: he was the perfect kid.

The bonds he formed proved pivotal when he went missing, as his friends and family bent over backwards to bring him home. Kidnapped by a Demogorgon and held captive in the Upside Down, we don't actually see much of him in the first season. Rather, we learn about him

through his friends and family. Known as 'Will The Wise' to his D&D 'party', Will uses his wisdom to his advantage – demonstrated when he learns to communicate with his mother across worlds using fairy lights.

Through the efforts of Sheriff Hopper and his mother, Will is rescued. However, his harrowing ordeal is never far from his mind. Will feels coddled by his friends and family, he's called 'Zombie Boy' at school, and soon learns that something much more malevolent than the Demogorgon has plans for him. Will has been possessed by the Mind Flayer, an otherworldly creature from the Upside Down.

As he tries to readjust to his life, he is plagued by glimpses of the gargantuan beast looming over Hawkins.

The Mind Flayer's hold over Will becomes so powerful it is able to speak through and control him. With the help of Jonathan, Joyce and Nancy, it is exorcised from Will's body, severing his connection to the Upside Down.

Will is more than happy to immerse himself in the worlds of D&D, comics and The Lord of the Rings – his reluctance to 'grow up' could be a lasting effect of the trauma he endured. This part of him causes a schism with his friends during the summer of 1985. They are too concerned with chasing girls, where Will just wants to cast himself as Dungeon Master.

A second incursion from the Mind Flayer brings the party back together once again, however, and Will uses his latent 'second sight' ability to sense the monster's presence.

Will finishes the summer saying farewell to his childhood and home comforts, as well as his actual home, when his family and Eleven choose to leave Hawkins behind for a more peaceful life in California.

Inevitably, things don't go to plan. When Eleven is abducted, Will and his friends are embroiled in yet another conflict with the Upside Down. With Will back in Hawkins with the friends he was so worried about drifting apart from, his otherworldly experiences are going to prove vital in defeating Vecna.

# Joyce Byers

## MEET THE MOTHER WHO WOULDN'T GIVE UP ON HER CHILD

WORDS **STEVE WRIGHT**

**T**he story of Joyce Byers (Winona Ryder) in *Stranger Things* begins with every mother's worst nightmare: her child going missing. It's this that drives the plot, but it's Joyce's refusal to lose hope that saves the day.

A dedicated mother to Jonathan and Will, Joyce has pretty much been left to man Fort Byers alone after the departure of her feckless ex-husband, Lonnie, so it would be understandable if she has a bit of a breakdown, as everyone assumes she has when she plasters the walls of her house with letters.

However, that's not true. Realising that Will is trapped and attempting to communicate with her, she provides him with a means to do so. Even when his 'body' is discovered in the nearby quarry, she refuses to believe he's dead. Getting former schoolfriend Hopper onside, she teams up with Eleven and her sons' friends, and ventures into the Upside Down to rescue Will. Celebrating a while later with Christmas dinner, all appears well.

However, it's not to be. While everyone seems to have moved on, with Joyce shacking up with another former schoolfriend, 'Superhero' Bob Newby, it becomes clear that Will is still experiencing visions of the Upside Down. When she is attacked by Demodogs at the Hawkins Lab, she is only just able to escape – Bob isn't so lucky.

Despite this devastating blow, Joyce is able to help exorcise the Mind Flayer from Will's body. So it's a bittersweet ending for Joyce – her son is safe, but she's lost someone she had real feelings for.

He isn't the only one, though. While her and Hopper have grown closer, she's understandably reluctant to commit. Regardless, there isn't much time to dwell, as there are more mysterious goings-on in Hawkins. The discovery of a hidden Russian base is inevitably connected to the Upside Down, and into another adventure they're pulled.

The chemistry between Joyce and Hopper continues to grow to the point where it seems like she might finally be acknowledging Murray's advice to "tear off those clothes and get it over with already", promising a dinner date with Hopper once it's all over.

Sadly, they never get the chance. With Hopper forced to stay behind in order to close the gate, he seemingly sacrifices himself to do so, leaving Joyce devastated once more.

As far as Hawkins is concerned, this is the final straw. Following through on her earlier plans, Joyce departs to Lenora Hills in California alongside her sons and Eleven.

Just as she seems to be settling into a life of normality, Joyce receives a package containing a Russian doll. Seeing this as a sign that Hopper is alive, she and a reluctant Murray head off to Siberia, where after a plane crash, encounters with Demodogs and lots of gunfire, her and Hopper are reunited – sealed with a kiss – before flying back to the US. Closing the season back in Hawkins with her family, it's good to have Joyce back.

# IRRESPONSIBLE? MAYBE. VIOLENT? POSSIBLY. HEROIC? CERTAINLY. POLICE CHIEF JIM HOPPER IS ABSOLUTELY HAWKINS' NUMBER-ONE LAWMAN

WORDS **DREW SLEEP**

The chief of police in Hawkins, we first encounter Jim Hopper (David Harbour) as he carries decades of demons on his back. An alcoholic chain smoker, the premature death of his daughter and collapse of his marriage sent the lawman on a downward spiral. The mundane life in Hawkins doesn't help; he can get away with oversleeping and abusing pills and the bottle... that is, until the case of Will Byers falls onto his desk.

Will's disappearance stirs a dormant dynamism in Hopper. It turns out that deep down, Hopper is the hero Hawkins needs. Capable, brave and compassionate, his drive to solve the mystery leads him down a rabbit hole of conspiracy and the supernatural – all of which has been happening under his nose. Confounding the case even further is the sudden appearance of a child who only goes by the name Eleven.

Hopper's brash, fist-first gumshoe approach to the mystery might not be conventional, but it gets results. After discovering Will's whereabouts, Hopper and Joyce travel to the Upside Down and rescue the young boy. His mission complete, Hopper chooses to take Eleven in, sheltering her from the shady scientists hunting her.

The two build a warm relationship, allowing the chief's past wounds to heal and giving her the father she deserves. However, his over-protectiveness pushes Eleven away. Meanwhile, the Upside Down's hold on Hawkins strengthens, and Hopper discovers a network of tunnels below the town that again puts him at odds with the scientists at Hawkins Lab.

After a confrontation with Mike Wheeler, Hopper realises he is too coddling of Eleven and reconciles with her – and just in time, too. He escorts his daughter below Hawkins to a gateway under Hawkins Lab to the Upside Down, where she seals the portal. With a forged birth certificate for 'Jane Hopper', Jim loosens his grip and lets her experience the life of a teenage girl.

In 1985, things kick off yet again. Hopper and Joyce embark on another fist fight-laden quest as they discover Russian agents working under the town. This time, however, Hopper's headstrong attitude gets the better of him, and he finds himself on the wrong side of a closing portal.

While his friends believe him dead, in reality he's been transported to the other end of the portal. Unfortunately, this happens to be a Russian gulag, where he spends a number of months being tortured before being put to work alongside the rest of the prisoners.

After befriending a prison guard, Dmitri, who manages to send a coded warning to Joyce, it looks like Hopper's escape will be straightforward. However, he's not off the hook yet. To say he's put through the mill is an understatement: he's recaptured, beaten up, and forced to fight Demogorgons. Still, it gives him a chance to show off his flamethrower skills and swordsmanship.

It all turns out to be worthwhile when he and Joyce are finally reunited – and 'will they, won't they?' becomes 'of course they do, was that even a question?'

Returning back to Hawkins to be reunited with Eleven, his arrival is marked by storm clouds forming. It's just as well that Hawkins has its sheriff back...

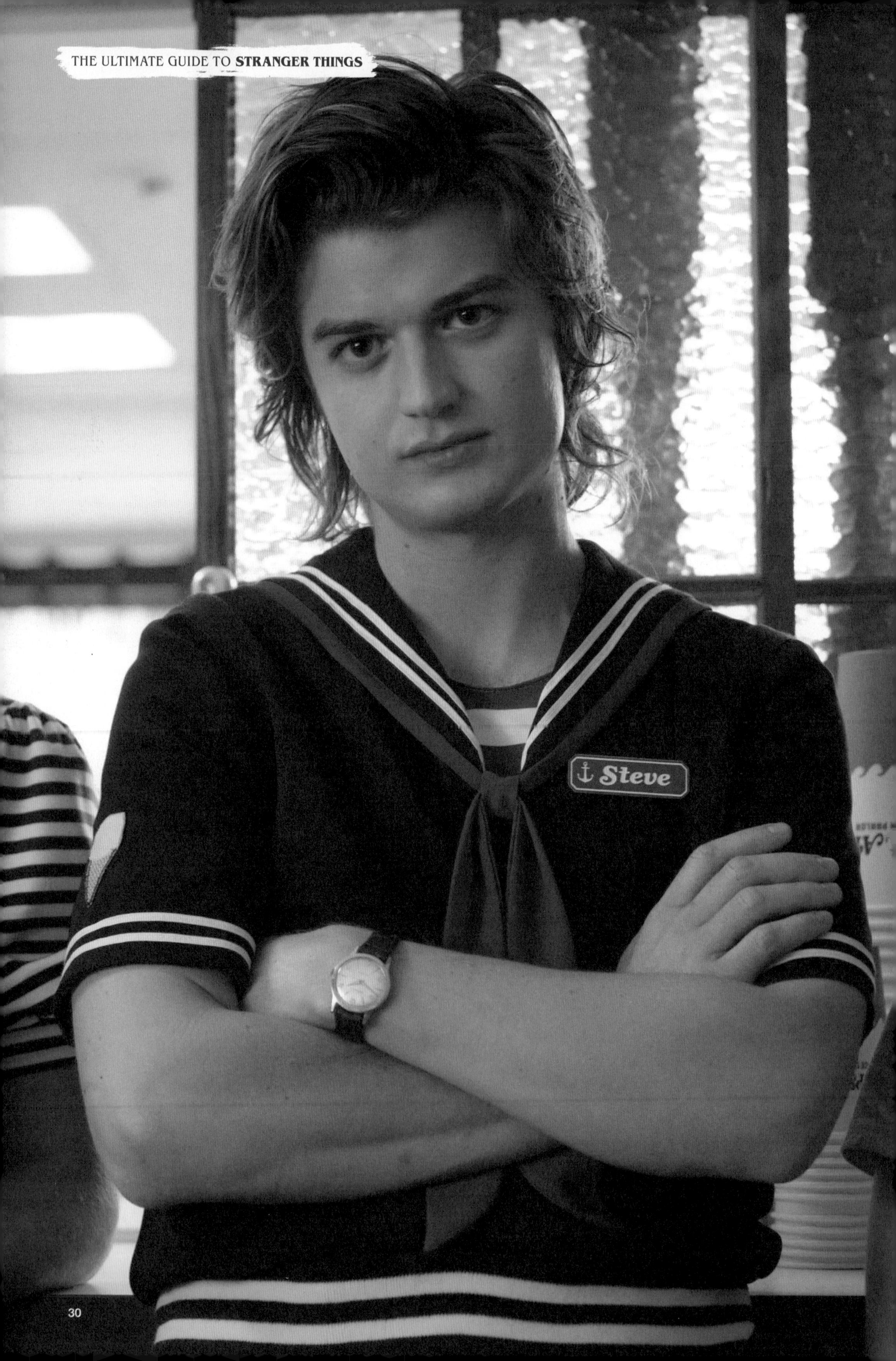
Steve

# Steve Harrington

## FROM HIGH SCHOOL ZERO TO BRAVE-HEARTED HERO, STEVE'S STORY IS ONE FOR HAWKINS HISTORIANS

WORDS **DREW SLEEP**

**W**e first meet Steve Harrington (Joe Keery) as the boyfriend of Nancy Wheeler. A stereotypical popular high-school kid, 'King Steve' appears mean, vapid and pushy. However, throughout the series, we see him evolve into a hero with a heart of gold who frequently takes one for the team.

In the first season, Steve is a reluctant antagonist. His insecurities often put him at odds with Nancy and high-school outcast Jonathan Byers. In an effort to maintain his stratospheric popularity with his peer-pressuring 'popular kid' crew, Steve talks down to and bullies those he considers beneath him.

Yet, after dining on some humble pie when Nancy leaves him, Steve rises to the mantle of hero when he helps Jonathan and Nancy defend the Byers' house from a Demogorgon. Spiked bat in hand, he battles the creature, giving Jonathan a chance to set the beast ablaze.

Afterwards, Steve reconciles with Nancy and even buys Jonathan a replacement camera, fully solidifying him as one of the good guys.

During the Mind Flayer crisis of 1984, Steve's personal life takes a nosedive. His school popularity is overthrown by Hawkins newcomer and all-around bad boy Billy Hargrove, and his relationship with Nancy fizzles out.

Steve finds a new purpose by bonding with Dustin Henderson. When the curly-haired kid enlists Steve to help 'deal' with his pet Demogorgon, Dart, our hero once again takes up his spiked baseball bat and makes a stand in a junkyard to defend Dustin's friends from a horde of Demodogs. Steve builds a rapport with the kids, especially Dustin, who he takes under his wing. This newfound parental instinct kicks into overdrive when he has to face down and subsequently take a pounding from his high-school nemesis, Billy, to protect his new pre-teen pals.

Steve finishes the season battered and down on his luck, but not alone. He finds a friend and surrogate brother in Dustin, and graduates high school – only to end up with poor grades and selling ice-cream at Scoops Ahoy.

Dressed in a sailor uniform and forced to endure a frosty working relationship with fellow Scoops Ahoy worker Robin Buckley, Steve suffers humiliation working at the Starcourt Mall in summer 1985.

But this is Hawkins, and there's always *something* lurking around the corner. In Steve's case, it's Russian spies. Teaming up with Robin, Dustin and Lucas Sinclair's sister Erica, Steve helps uncover a red scare right under the mall. In the process, he takes another knuckle sandwich to the face from a Russian brute during an interrogation session, but finds a kindred spirit in Robin, and ends up taking up a better job with her at Hawkins Family Video.

He continues to put himself in harm's way to help his friends, damn near getting eaten alive in the Upside Down – all the while hopes of a reunion with Nancy continue to get dangled before abuptly getting yanked away.

It always seems to be a 'you lose some, you win some' situation with Steve, and that's perhaps why we like him so much. Following his redemption arc in season one, he has managed to turn a bad situation on its head multiple times. There's no way you can't be drawn to King Steve.

# WHETHER SHE'S ARMED WITH A BASEBALL BAT, FIREWORKS OR A TAPE RECORDER, YOU WOULDN'T WANT TO BET AGAINST NANCY WHEELER

WORDS **STEVE WRIGHT**

Perhaps more than anyone else in the series – apart from Steve Harrington – Nancy Wheeler (Natalia Dyer) presents the best example of Stranger Things' ability to turn first impressions on their head.

Initially presented as Mike's intelligent yet easily led elder sister, Nancy has evolved over the course of the show to arguably become its moral centre: unwilling to let things go when just about everyone else has given up.

It's a bit of a journey to get to this point, though. Not that she's a bad person; she just does what a lot of teenagers do: ignore her parents, argue with her brother and lie about where she's going in order to hook up with the boy she likes.

However, in the world of Stranger Things, mistakes seem to be punished more harshly, as we see with the fate of Nancy's best friend Barb. Having been cast aside at a poolhouse meet-up, Nancy is occupied while her best friend is killed by the Demogorgon.

Finally coming to her senses, she teams up with Jonathan to investigate Barb's disappearance, playing a vital role in locating the Demogorgon – and Will Byers, in the process – although this confirms the death of Barb.

Guilt-ridden, Nancy breaks up with Steve, later teaming up with Jonathan once more while they trick Dr Owens into disclosing the truth of what happened to Barb. Mission accomplished, they once again help save the day, restraining Will as the Mind Flayer is exorcised from him.

Season three begins on a high for Nancy – she's with Jonathan, justice for Barb has been achieved, and she's even cheered up Dustin at the Snow Ball.

However, her positivity is brought crashing down by her experiences as an intern at the Hawkins Post. Jeered at by her misogynistic male colleagues, it's only a timely pep talk from her mother, Karen, that gets her back on her feet.

What results is a catharsis of sorts, as while continuing with their investigation, Nancy and Jonathan face off against mind-flayed versions of their horrible former co-workers, ultimately defeating them, before taking part in the battle at Starcourt Mall.

However, it's a bittersweet ending, with Jonathan leaving Hawkins with his family. Granted, it's not the saddest moment in an episode peppered with sad moments, but it's still gutting to see the young lovers separated. A few months down the line, though, and they appear to be getting on just fine: Nancy is editor of the Hawkins student paper, and is too busy to go visit Jonathan at spring break. But a string of grisly, Upside Down-linked murders – one victim being her classmate, Fred – has her teaming up with Steve, Robin and co to investigate what's going on.

It's all going on for Nancy: from surviving a direct assault from Vecna, to facing the possible rekindling of her feelings towards Steve. Still, if she can continue to bounce back as well as she can wield a shotgun, we're sure she will be just fine.

©Alamy

33

# Max Mayfield

## A VIDEOGAME VIRTUOSO, STAR SKATER AND FIERCE FRIEND, MAX WILL ALWAYS HAVE YOUR BACK

WORDS **DREW SLEEP**

In October 1984, the local arcade hummed with excitement as a newcomer smashed high-score records on the videogame machines. Their calling card? The name MADMAX proudly displayed at the top of the high-score screen.

This was the alias used by Maxine Mayfield (Sadie Sink), who had moved from California to Hawkins, Indiana, with her mother, stepfather and rage-filled stepbrother, Billy Hargrove. Her impressive gaming skills drew the attention of Dustin and Lucas, who invited her to join their 'Party'. While Max's relationship with the group was unsteady at first, she soon demonstrated her worth to the crew by helping them hunt down Dustin's pet Demogorgon, Dart, and later saved Steve Harrington from a near-fatal beating from Billy by stabbing her stepbrother with a sedative.

Skilled with a skateboard, lockpick and behind the wheel of a car, Max is the natural rogue (or "zoomer", in her own words) of the Party. She is fiercely protective of her friends – in particular, she keeps Eleven close and helps introduce her to the life of a teenager. She also has a soft spot for Lucas and struck up a romantic relationship with him after they kissed at the Snow Ball – the pair have been lovebirds ever since.

Despite their fraught relationship, and after all the hurt he caused, Max did love her stepbrother. After his redemptive self-sacrifice saving the Party from the Spider Monster at the Starcourt Mall, we see Max mourning Billy months after his demise. This demonstrates Max's most admirable trait: her empathy and loyalty to those she loves. You'd do well to have MADMAX on your side.

As it turns out, Max's troubles are just beginning. Grieving the loss of her stepbrother and the subsequent break-up of her family, and having pushed Lucas away, she finds herself easy prey for the new threat of Vecna, who targets those with traumatic pasts.

Unlike his previous victims, however, Max isn't alone. Assisted by her friends – not to mention a certain Kate Bush – she goes running up that hill all the way out of the Upside Down, becoming the first of those targeted by the series' big bad to escape with their life.

But again, it appears that Max's journey towards a happy ending is a fraught one. When the plan to lure Vecna into a trap goes horribly wrong, Max is brutally attacked by the monster, dying in Lucas's arms in one world before Eleven can save her from getting severely mutilated in the other.

While Eleven ultimately manages to bring her back to some sort of life, she remains in a coma, with only the most basic signs of life. Even El can't detect any signs of her subsconsciousness in the Void.

This can't be the end for Max – it would simply be far too cruel a way to go, especially considering what she has already been through. Fingers crossed that she finds a way back to the world of the living.

©Alamy

# Karen Wheeler

## THE WHEELER FAMILY MATRIARCH BALANCES HER CHALLENGING FAMILY WITH HER YEARNING FOR SOME EXCITEMENT IN HER OWN LIFE

WORDS **STEVE WRIGHT**

**W**ife to Ted, and mother to Nancy, Mike and Holly, Karen Wheeler (Cara Buono) dotes on her family – not that she gets much appreciation for it. When the series starts, Nancy is often off with her new friends, and Mike is preoccupied with looking for Will and hiding Eleven, leaving Karen to man fort Wheeler with little Holly on her hip.

With the borderline oblivious Ted largely leaving the parental duties to Karen, she has to do the bulk of the parenting groundwork, making her seem overbearing as a result. For the most part, her pleas for them to talk to her fall on death ears.

Having married Ted young, the flames of passion have died out in their marriage long ago, which makes it understandable – if ill-advised – when Karen reacts positively to the flirtations of Billy Hargrove when he comes knocking for his sister.

Having invested in a new hairdo – and swimsuit – she successfully catches his eye at the local swimming pool once more, and arranges a secret rendezvous. However, at the last moment her conscience gets the better of her, and she backs out. This is probably just as well, since Billy has been possessed by the Mind Flayer by this point.

Despite almost making a bad decision, she's there for her children when they need her the most, giving Nancy a timely pep talk after her firing from the *Hawkins Post*, and comforting Mike when Will and El leave Hawkins.

So, in summary: not perfect by any means, but a good mother when it matters.

© Alamy

## "DO YOU WANNA BE NORMAL? DO YOU WANNA BE JUST LIKE EVERYONE ELSE? BEING A FREAK IS THE BEST. I'M A FREAK!"

WORDS **ALICE PATTILLO**

When Will's older brother arrives home late from work in the first season's pilot, he couldn't imagine the repercussions his extended shift would have. As Will is catapulted into the Upside Down, the crisis brings intelligent, introverted Jonathan (Charlie Heaton) out of his shell.

Season one sees him step up as a big brother when Will is missing, uncharacteristically challenge Steve Harrington to a fist-fight, stand up to his abusive father Lonnie and ultimately face off with the monsters of the Upside Down. Jonathan's a keen photographer, perceptively commenting that, "Sometimes people don't really say what they're thinking. But you capture the right moment... it says more." He is passionate about music, introducing Will to The Clash and compiling a mixtape with the likes of David Bowie and Joy Division.

Where he excels in the arts, however, he's less capable when it comes to social interactions, preferring solitude. Jonathan might be shy, but he's brave, loyal and comfortable being an outsider; he follows his own path, encouraging Will to do the same. While he might show a general disdain for others, he is devoted to those he loves, particularly his brother. Jonathan shows his kindness and compassion through actions rather than words.

It's clear how much he has progressed: he has a girlfriend in the form of his long-term crush, Nancy, and has finally made a non-familiar pal in the form of stoner Argyle. He may be unsure what he wants, but he seems to be adept at making the right decision.

© Alamy

# Dr Martin Brenner

## PAPA'S RUTHLESSLY AMBITIOUS APPROACH TO SCIENCE IS RESPONSIBLE FOR ALL THE CHAOS INFLICTED UPON HAWKINS

WORDS **ALICE PATTILLO**

The closest thing El had to a father figure before Hopper, Martin Brenner (Matthew Modine) is a brilliant yet immoral scientist. As director of Hawkins National Laboratory he began experimenting on college students – one of whom was Terry Ives – in order to develop mind-control techniques.

After discovering that Terry was pregnant he stole her baby, Jane, and raised her in the lab, giving her the number 011 and studying the psychokinetic abilities she developed due to the experiments he had subjected her mother to. He displays highly manipulative traits and very little empathy or consideration for others. As Papa, he would regularly put El through cruel psychological torture, despite her being a child, and never gave her any love or socialisation.

Brenner has a lot to answer for: opening the gate to the Upside Down, and releasing the monstrous creatures and toxic biological matter as he encourages El to make contact with the Demogorgon when spying on a Russian agent in the void. He is unscrupulous and shows a total disregard for human life. In an attempt to cover up the repercussions of his work, he faked Will Byers' death and is keen to let the chaos continue in Hawkins as long as it advances his scientific understanding.

While he later appears to have perished in a Demogorgon attack, he is then revealed to have survived, bringing El back into the fold once more as he helps her to get her powers back in order to combat Vecna (a threat he himself is responsible for). While he ultimately sacrifices himself to save El, all her problems start with him.

# Bob Newby

## HIS STAY ON THE SHOW WAS SHORT-LIVED, BUT NO ONE WILL EVER FORGET BOB NEWBY SUPERHERO

WORDS **STEVE WRIGHT**

**A**lso known as 'Bob Newby Superhero', Bob (Sean Astin) is one of those rare examples of a person who genuinely is what they seem: an authentic and wholehearted individual who will go out of his way to help others.

A former classmate of Jim Hopper and Joyce Byers, he ends up dating the latter in season three. He was also the founder of the Hawkins Middle AV Club that the boys participate in. Basically, it's thanks to his early efforts that they were able to save Will!

As well as being a devoted boyfriend to Joyce, he does his best to be there for Will, always being on hand for advice (even if some of this is questionable – turns out the Mind Flayer doesn't take kindly to being told to "Go away").

The way events transpire, Bob plays a key role in the events of the third season, working out where Hopper is trapped by deciphering Will's drawings, and drawing on his knowledge of BASIC to turn the power in the lab back on and rescue everyone. Sadly, his heroic actions come at the cost of his own life, as his escape from the facility is foiled by a group of Demodogs. Such a beloved character really did not deserve to die in such a gruesome way.

So while Bob is no more, he lives on both in our hearts, and on Will's 'Bob Newby Superhero' drawing that he affixes to the Byers family refrigerator.

# Billy Hargrove

## THE GANG'S FORMER TORMENTOR BECOMES SEASON 3'S MAIN ANTAGONIST, ONLY TO TRAGICALLY REDEEM HIMSELF

WORDS **ALICE PATTILLO**

Introduced in Stranger Things' second season, Billy Hargrove (Dacre Montgomery) moves to Hawkins with his step-sister Max. Billy is a bully, attempting to control and intimidate Max, her friends and anyone else who gets in his way.

Pulling up to school in a blue Camaro and striking up a rivalry with Steve Harrington, his bad boy persona and fit physique gets him noticed by the ladies, but he displays a misogynistic attitude, hooking up with a new girl every day, attempting to start an affair with Mrs Wheeler and commenting to Steve that "there are always other bitches" when his relationship with Nancy is on the rocks.

At times, however, Billy shows glimpses of care and a protective instinct towards his step-sister Max, even if his way of showing it comes over as toxic and controlling.

When the Mind Flayer implants part of itself in Billy's brain in season three, he accrues an army of followers, who are all possessed by the Flayer in its attempt to annihilate everyone. When El accesses Billy's memories, we witness his last true moment of happiness – surfing with his mother. Before she left due to his father's abuse, he was a happy and friendly boy, and it is revealed that he only became a bully when the violence his dad inflicted upon her was transferred onto him. It is the happy memory of his mother that El uses to reignite the humanity in Billy, and he ultimately sacrifices himself to save the gang, gasping "I'm sorry" to Max before taking his last breath.

His death leaves a lasting impact, particularly on Max, with her grief at his demise leaving her easy prey for the threat of Vecna.

© Alamy

## STRANGER THINGS' UNOFFICIAL LOVE DOCTOR IS ALSO THE SHOW'S UNSPOKEN HERO

WORDS **STEVE WRIGHT**

**A** former investigative journalist, when we meet him, Murray Bauman (Brett Gelman) is working as a private investigator, having been hired by Barb's parents to look into their daughter's disappearance.

Living in a run-down shack in Illinois, Murray isn't taken seriously by most due to his eccentricity and lack of regard for dress, personal hygiene or social niceties, but this demeanour hides a shrewd and sharp individual with a strong sense of duty.

For a start, he seems to be spot-on about almost anything. He predicts the Russian spy presence in Hawkins a long time before anyone else notices, and exasperatedly points out when couples are a match even before they themselves

are fully aware of it – first with Nancy and Jonathan, and then again with Joyce and Hopper.

He later gives Nancy and Jonathan some advice in order to help get the lab shut down – a success he's later to bask in.

A year later, he's back helping out Hopper and Joyce in interrogating Russian prisoner Alexei – who despite his suspicions regarding his country of birth, he later bonds with – before accompanying the trio to the fair and later the mall, in their attempts to get the portal shut down.

The following summer, he continues to go above and beyond, travelling with Joyce to Russia to rescue Hopper. Yep, it's fair to say that Bauman is the unsung hero of the show.

41

# Dr Sam Owens

## WHEN IT'S GAME OVER FOR DR BRENNER, UP STEPS DR OWENS

WORDS **STEVE WRIGHT**

The successor to the nefarious Dr Brenner as Director of Operations at Hawkins Lab, Dr Sam Owens (Paul Reiser) isn't the outright villain his predecessor was.

Sure, he's determined to keep the Upside Down a secret, and he isn't averse to working for a shady government agency with a vaguely defined purpose, but he has perfectly legitimate reasons for keeping the Upside Down under wraps – namely, what would happen if certain governments had access to it.

He's also a hell of a lot nicer to his patients – while Brenner put Eleven through hell, he's a lot more careful with Will (although he's not averse to putting him through the odd telepathic burning session).

Regardless, he shows by his actions that he's not completely in it for himself, first by risking death in order to make sure that Joyce and Hopper make it out the lab safely when they're threatened by the Demodogs. But his finest moment comes when he provides Eleven with a forged birth certificate cementing her status as Hopper's daughter. He may not have had any involvement in her mistreatment, but it's nice to see someone making amends.

Having helped Eleven and the Byers family relocate after the attack on the Starcourt Mall, he returns to recruit her once more in the face of Vecna's threat, teaming up with the still-alive Brenner. However, having been captured after Sullivan and his forces invade the lab, his fate is very much up in the air.

# Robin Buckley

## THE SCOOPS AHOY EMPLOYEE COVERS HER TRUE FEELINGS WITH A VENEER OF SARCASM

WORDS **STEVE WRIGHT**

**F**irst arriving on the show as Steve Harrington's co-worker at Scoops Ahoy, Robin (Maya Hawke) has a history with 'Dingus' that he is completely oblivious to.

At first, she couldn't appear anymore different to him; he's all about his reputation and reliving past glories, while Robin, having no reputation to speak of, is far more at ease with saying whatever she wants.

Initially taking pleasure in mocking Steve during their working hours, she eventually gets drawn into his and Dustin's investigation into the source of the Russian transmissions, with her language skills proving to be a vital asset in decoding what is being said.

While she's arguably a bit irresponsible (along with Steve, of course) in allowing Dustin and Erica to get caught up in what is in reality an extremely dangerous situation, she shows bravery in facing up to the menacing Russian agents. All the while, it's clear that her mockery of Steve and frequent sarcasm is overcompensating for something.

Facing interrogation and truth serum, Robin and Steve finally reveal their deepest secrets to each other. Steve loves Robin, and Robin loves... another girl. Despite Steve's surprise, he's completely accepting of Robin's revelation, and her coming out only serves to deepen their bond.

Once the crisis is over, the two remain close friends, with Robin even helping Steve to get another job at the Family Video Store. He tries to return the favour the following summer, giving her advice when she notices pretty classmate Vickie. Still, romance might be on the backburner for now...

# Erica Sinclair

## THERE'S MORE TO HER THAN JUST ANNOYING HER OLDER BROTHER

WORDS **STEVE WRIGHT**

The stereotypical annoying younger sister, Erica (Priah Ferguson) likes nothing more than showing her brother Lucas as much disrespect as possible. Whether it be using his stuff without permission or calling him a nerd, she delights in giving him a hard time.

Laughing at his *Ghostbusters* costume? Check. Listening in on his radio chat? Check. Mocking his prom outfit and practice asking-out attempts? Check, check and check.

By the events of season three, she takes on a more important role in proceedings, assisting Steve, Dustin and Robin in their attempts to uncover the mystery of what's going on in the mall. Her actions are far from selfless, however; she just wants some free ice cream.

In the process, she shows she's not all mouth: faced with the possibility of death at the hands of Russian agents, she's more annoyed at the prospect of missing out on a sleepover.

For all her mocking of Lucas and his friends, however, she has serious nerd credentials herself: her *My Little Pony* knowledge is second to none. Plus, she's not exactly displeased at being left the gang's old Dungeons & Dragons sets, putting her skills to the test when she stands in for her brother at the Hellfire Club while he's off playing basketball.

For all her rivalries with her brother, she's firmly on his side when it matters, even putting herself in harm's way when satanic panic-afflicted jocks come knocking.

With the threat of Vecna still present, Erica's sure to play a key role in what's up ahead.

# THE MISUNDERSTOOD METALHEAD TOUCHED THE HEARTS OF EVERYONE WHO GOT TO KNOW HIM

WORDS **STEVE WRIGHT**

**J**ust when you thought *Stranger Things* didn't have room for any more loveable underdogs, in knee slides Eddie Munson (Joseph Quinn), devil's horns pointing to the sky.

On first appearances, it's hard to know what to make of him. As the head of Hawkins High School's Dungeons & Dragons hideaway, the Hellfire Club, Dustin and Mike seem to be both in awe of and slightly scared of him, and it's easy to see why. Caring more about gaming, metal and providing a sanctuary for the school's fellow misfits, he seems utterly unafraid of judgement from his peers and is scathing of social norms.

However, this is all put to the test when haunted cheerleader Chrissy Cunningham is brutally murdered before his eyes. Helpless and traumatised, he flees, only coming back to his senses when Dustin and co manage to catch up with him.

Regardless, thanks to the ravings of vengeful school jock Jason Carver, Eddie is blamed for the murders and becomes a target of a full-blown satanic panic in Hawkins. But even with this going on, Eddie shows his true colours as a good person, helping the gang attempt to combat Vecna's plans and bonding with Steve over Dustin.

Ultimately, his bravery costs him his life. Having initially distracted the creatures of the Upside Down with a stirring rendition of 'Master of Puppets', he sacrifices all by luring them away, protecting his friends and adding to Metallica's bank balance.

So, in short, he's the hero the majority of Hawkins doesn't realise it has. Hopefully his sacrifice won't be in vain.

# Henry Creel

## BEFORE HE EVOLVED INTO VECNA, HENRY CREEL'S FACADE OF INNOCENCE FOOLED EVERYONE... UNTIL IT WAS TOO LATE

WORDS **STEVE WRIGHT**

When we first hear of Henry Creel (Raphael Luce), he's a mere footnote to the tragic tale of his father, Victor. Believed by the rest of the world to have been just one victim of a murderous rampage, he is quickly forgotten about.

Yet, in true *Stranger Things* fashion, nothing is what it seems. When an orderly by the name of Peter Ballard (Jamie Campbell Bower) is seen helping Eleven relive her early years at the Hawkins National Laboratory, we know something isn't quite right about him, but nothing prepares us for the truth.

As it turns out, Peter is in fact Henry. Born with the powers of telekinesis and telepathy, he quickly grows disgusted with humanity, and murders his mother and sister, framing his father for the killings. Unschooled in his abilities, however, his weakened state leaves him easy prey for a certain Dr Brenner, who brings him into the lab, labels him '001', and subdues him with a device designed to suppress his powers.

Having tricked Eleven into removing it, Henry unleashes his powers, slaughtering most of the staff and his fellow test subjects, before attempting to do the same to El when she refuses to join him.

As with others who have tried to defeat El, this doesn't actually go too well for him. After being caught off guard by her abilities, he is transported to the Upside Down, distorting his appearance beyond recognition and turning him into the physical manifestation of the monster he already was.

## JONATHAN'S STONER BUDDY PROVIDES THE TRANSPORT – AND THE SUBSTANCE(S) – IN THE FOURTH SEASON

WORDS **STEVE WRIGHT**

The introduction of Argyle (Eduardo Franco) in season four represents the filling of a gaping dearth we're surprised remained open for so long in an '80s-set show: the stoner best friend.

This isn't the only role he fulfils, however; upon the Byers' move to California, he quickly becomes best friends with Jonathan. For both of them, they may be the only friend of their own age they've ever had.

Jonathan isn't the chattiest, which is just as well, because Argyle can't stop. When he's not talking or working as a delivery boy for Surfer Boy Pizza, his primary interest is smoking industrial amounts of weed, something Jonathan himself seems to have taken to like a duck to water.

There's more to Argyle than first meets the eye, however. First off, rather than expressing any kind of jealousy for his new best friend's relationship with Nancy, he chastises him for lying to her. Secondly, he drives headlong into danger – albeit unwittingly – when he rescues everyone from the shoot-out at the Byers' house, although he does willingly get involved in saving Eleven.

While he hasn't interacted with a huge amount of the cast yet, save for Mike, Eleven and the Byers family, we're sure they'll get along famously – after all, it took mere minutes of being in his company for Suzie's sister, Eden, to happily share a bong with him. With the threat of the Upside Down ever closer, we suspect that he'll be embracing the magic dragon even more often.

# Creatures of the Upside Down

## THIS WORLD IS HOME TO SOME DANGEROUS RESIDENTS. YOU BETTER HOPE YOU DON'T MEET THESE CREEPY CREATURES ON A DARK NIGHT

WORDS **DREW SLEEP**

Existing parallel to our world, the Upside Down is a dimension that defines danger. As you take uneasy steps across its stagnant environment, you might find friendly locales like Castle Byers or the library. Don't let that familiarity fool you, however. The Upside Down is uncanny, unpleasant and unwelcoming, and you'd do well to stay far, far away.

This alien landscape is home to grotesque abominations that consider humans their prey. These creatures only exist to kill and dominate – there is no reasoning with them, no bargaining; all you can do is run, fight back, or perish.

Our world became entangled with the Upside Down in 1983 when the scientists at Hawkins National Laboratory created a gateway between the two worlds. The scientists discovered that one of their test subjects – Eleven – had encountered an otherworldly creature in an experiment. In forcing the girl to make contact with this being, a rift was created, and the entity called a Demogorgon stumbled through.

This was the first known incursion of a creature from the Upside Down entering our world, and it would not be the last. We later learn that there is an intelligent and malevolent force pulling the strings. One which has designs on our world and will stop at nothing to dominate the human race. The creatures of the Upside Down are still enshrouded in mystery. However, here are the entities we know and what they're capable of...

**Above:** The Demogorgon unfurls its flower-like maw to reveal row upon row of terrifying teeth.

# "As vicious as they are, the Demogorgons are far from the most menacing lifeform of the Upside Down"

## THE DEMOGORGON

The first creature of the Upside Down we encounter in the *Stranger Things* canon is the Demogorgon. It's also the species of monster we know the most about, having explored its entire life cycle across four seasons. It's a tall, grey, thin humanoid figure with super-strong elongated limbs and a featureless face. The stuff of nightmares, basically. And that featureless head? It unfurls like a flower, revealing rows of sharp teeth and a gaping maw. The Demogorgon is named after a Dungeons & Dragons monster. In the tabletop game, it's a powerful fiend that defeats Will Byers' in-game character, foreshadowing his abduction in the real world.

This creature is truly not of this world, uncanny, uncaring and nigh-on unstoppable. That escaped Demogorgon from Hawkins Lab we mentioned earlier gets beaten, shot and set on fire, yet it still manages to draw breath until Eleven obliterates it with her psychic powers.

It acts as an instinctive predator, killing what it deems to be prey, yet it appears to have desires beyond this. Instead of killing him, it abducts Will Byers and cocoons him in the Upside Down, perhaps to use him to create another Demogorgon in a Xenomorph-style reproductive ritual.

Sticking with the Xenomorph comparison, much like the star from the *Alien* films, the Demogorgon goes through different forms throughout its life. We have Dustin Henderson to thank for this information, as he attempts to keep one of these otherworldly horrors as a pet, and we get to watch it grow. The first stage looks like a chunky slug and potentially requires a host to grow. After his ordeal

in the Upside Down, Will coughs one of these up into his bathroom sink.

Stage two, or the 'Pollywog', looks similar to a newt... or, you know, a pollywog. Here, we can see an instinct to feed kick in. Dustin's creature, Dart, steals candy and rummages around trash cans, for example. A fear of fire also surfaces at this point.

The third stage clearly resembles a frog. The monster's skin turns a bottle-green, it grows rapidly and fully walks on its four legs. You'll start to see tiny rows of pointed teeth at this stage, too. Perhaps this cute thing is not that friendly, after all?

Stages four and five are fairly similar to each other. Here, the Demogorgon resembles a slimy alien cat or dog... only instead of a cute furry face, it has that god-awful mouth flower. After the fifth stage of growth is complete, the Demogorgon becomes bigger, bipedal and fully develops into that gross beastie we know and love. Gorgeous.

## THE MIND FLAYER

As vicious as they are, the Demogorgons are far from the most menacing lifeform of the Upside Down. That honour belongs to the Mind Flayer, a Lovecraftian aberration of gigantic proportions. Even its name elicits a feeling of existential dread: this creature will peel away everything about you until there is nothing left. Again, this creature is named after a similarly grotesque D&D creature, one that takes great pride in devouring the brains of other humanoid creatures.

**Left:** A gateway to the Upside Down – an unpleasant and unwelcoming parallel world.

**Left:** Billy finds himself possessed by the Mind Flayer.

**Right:** Hopper explores the underground tunnels of the Upside Down.

Unlike the Demogorgons that appear to operate purely on instinct, the Mind Flayer is intelligent. It schemes, manipulates and is highly hostile to the human race. We only ever see the creature in the Upside Down, from the perspective of Will Byers, who shares a connection with the entity. It is massive; hundreds of feet tall, and its body comprises an ethereal, smoke-like substance. It stands astride multiple tendrils that split off into countless 'legs', resembling the roots and webbing that coat the entirety of its homeworld. At the centre of its tangle is a long, featureless head.

While its form is imposing, the Mind Flayer does not demonstrate any obvious physical threat like its Demogorgon sibling. Rather, this creature's weapon of choice is its psychic powers. It can dominate the minds of humans, twisting them and turning them into 'the Flayed'. We see the Mind Flayer attempt this with Will Byers, as it influences his mind making the sweet boy hostile to his friends and family. We also see it hold full control over the Demogorgons, ordering them to enact its will.

This mastermind's true motivations are unknown. Through his possession, Will offers a glimpse of the creature's plans. Speaking through Will, it tells us that it wishes to merge the Upside Down and our world together, granting it a larger dominion for it to rule over. Viewing itself as an apex predator, it will likely not stop until it dominates every living creature it can.

The Mind Flayer can also alter organic material and create proxies to do its bidding in our world. After the gate between worlds is reopened by Russian agents operating in Hawkins, the Mind Flayer dominates a group of rats and humans, morphing their matter into a real-world avatar. We see an even lesser, 'fleshy' version of the creature appear in Hawkins Hospital, created from a pair of Flayed humans with the objective of killing Nancy Wheeler and

Jonathan Byers. This iteration of the Mind Flayer is crab-like, rabid and susceptible to the remarkable superhuman powers of Eleven.

While the Mind Flayer is supremely powerful, it's not unstoppable. As with other creatures of the Upside Down, it holds an impulsive fear of fire and extends this phobia to its Flayed hosts. By placing a Flayed Will in a heated environment – surrounded by heaters and blankets – the Mind Flayer squirms in pain and discomfort, and ultimately tears itself from Will's body.

The victories against the Mind Flayer have been small and probably insignificant in the grand scheme of things. It still has plans for our world, and will likely regroup and return, perhaps more powerful than before.

## THE SPIDER MONSTER

The Mind Flayer casts a long shadow over Hawkins, but its true form only operates from its home realm, the Upside Down. Instead of entering our world, it chooses to operate through proxies. The 'Spider Monster' residing in the derelict steel works building is one of the Mind Flayer's avatars, and it is one heck of a grotesque monster.

Constructed from the flesh of Flayed rats and humans, the Mind Flayer twists organic matter from the creatures it dominates into its own image: an arachnid-like being with sinewy appendages. It has one objective: kill Eleven,

the one person standing between the Mind Flayer and Hawkins. It's not as imposing as its 'parent'. The Spider Monster stands at around 30 feet tall, with bones and teeth sticking out of its gross form. While the Mind Flayer is a creature evolved to fight mental battles, the Spider Monster is a physical powerhouse. Strong, vile and dangerous, it's a huge threat to the heroes of Hawkins.

Threatening as it might be, this is still a creature that requires an open connection to the Upside Down – and so the Mind Flayer – to survive. Once Jim Hopper destroyed the Russian-built gateway to the otherworldly dimension, the Mind Flayer's influence was severed, and so the Spider Monster melted away.

## THE FLAYED

Though they're 'technically' still human, the thralls of the Mind Flayer are so far removed from the people they once were it's difficult to see them as anything but monsters. The Flayed are stripped of all their worldly wants and desires, and only exist to serve the hive mind.

The Mind Flayer's influence twists its hosts' insides, and Flayed creatures no longer eat food. Instead, the Mind Flayer prefers that they consume poisonous chemicals like fertiliser and washing powder. A Flayed's blood turns a dark, tar-like colour too, which can be seen from their gross varicose veins.

**Left:** Steve battles the Demogorgon with his spiked bat.

**Right:** Eleven defeated a Demogorgon in *Stranger Things'* first season.

**Below:** Will is abducted and held hostage in the Upside Down.

**Left:** Meet Vecna, the series' real big bad all along.

A Flayed is nothing but a tool to the Mind Flayer; a being to be contorted to its master's ends. As such, the mastermind of the Upside Down can break down a Flayed into a fleshy sludge, morphing its thralls together into something much more insidious. We see this with the 'Spider Monster', being formed under the Hawkins steelworks, constructed from the flesh of hundreds of Flayed humans and rats.

As hopeless as it might seem, a Flayed can regain its humanity. Will Byers is fully rescued from the Mind Flayer's grasp, and while potentially too far gone to be fully saved, a Flayed Billy Hargrove regains his faculties just in time to save his sister and her friends.

## VECNA

The puppet master pulling the strings. Continuing with the D&D theme, Vecna's name comes from one of the game's greatest villains, and he does his evil legacy justice.

Given his final form when Eleven banishes him to the Upside Down, the twisted remnants of Henry Creel wastes no time in turning the hellish environment to his advantage, creating the Mind Flayer and orchestrating the events of much of the series.

Despite the otherworldly nature of the Upside Down, it's deeply ironic that the entire reason it's threatening mankind is because of a manmade problem: Creel was always a monster, but it was the intervention of Dr Brenner and co that gave him the tools to threaten humanity.

Possessing Creel's powers of telepathy and telekenesis, which he wields to brutal effect on Chrissy Cunningham, Fred Benson, Patrick McKinney and Max Mayfield, he is not invincible, as attacks by Eleven, Nancy and co show.

Even so, he's still at large. Going into season five, the final battle with him will be an epic like no other.

# The Seasons

# Season One

## MEET THE CAST – AND CREATURE! – THAT STARTED IT ALL. DO YOU DARE ENTER THE UPSIDE DOWN?

WORDS **JOEL McIVER**

**W**elcome to the dark but wonderful universe of season one of *Stranger Things*, the eight classic episodes from 2016 that set up the show's six-year run to date. From the moment that we find ourselves transported to the picture-postcard town of Hawkins, Indiana, in late 1983, we're placed directly into the centre of a web of characters, all leading very different lives, but all about to be drawn into a terrifying drama that is unlike any we've witnessed before.

Created by Ross and Matt Duffer, who learned their craft from *The Sixth Sense* director M Night Shyamalan, *Stranger Things* was utterly convincing for viewers of any age. Older fans who remembered the Eighties responded to the Duffer brothers' warm portrayal of pre-internet, pre-cellphone life in the suburbs, but you don't need to be aged over 40 to enjoy the vibes from that simpler age. Besides, who doesn't empathise with the gang of misfit kids at the heart of the *Stranger Things* universe? After all, we *were* those kids.

No wonder this amazing new show became a must-watch that year, competing with Netflix's established programming and scooping a ton of positive reviews from the critics. Suddenly, everyone wanted in on the *Stranger Things* phenomenon. Let's look back and remind ourselves how it unfolded...

©Alamy

**Above:** Jim Hopper, responsible for law and order in Hawkins, doesn't need monsters; he has inner demons of his own.

**Right:** Be grateful that the can isn't your head, because Eleven is about to crush it with telekinesis.

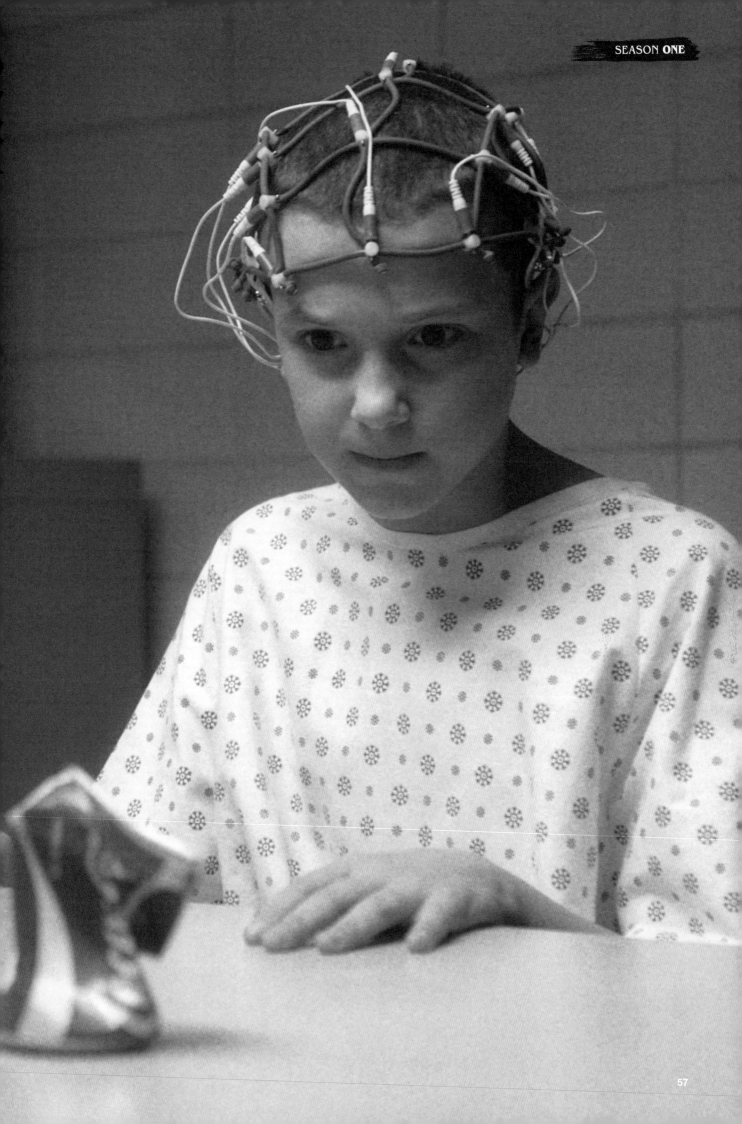

## CHAPTER ONE:
## THE VANISHING OF WILL BYERS

Don't all epic TV shows start with an unforgettable opening scene? In the case of *Stranger Things*' first episode, you'll never forget the moment that we enter a government-owned science facility in the – sadly fictional – town of Hawkins, Indiana. This being November 1983, when digital watches were pretty much the most advanced technology around, you won't see any recognisably modern gadgetry. As we look around the spooky facility, we know from the first few seconds that we really shouldn't be in here. This certainty deepens when a scientist is attacked by some horrendous-sounding monster: we say horrendous-'sounding', because in true sci-fi-horror style, we don't get to see the nasty thing yet.

We then meet Will Byers (Noah Schnapp), a local 12-year-old who is about to leave the weekly Dungeons & Dragons session that he plays with his friends Mike Wheeler (Finn Wolfhard), Dustin Henderson (Gaten Matarazzo) and Lucas Sinclair (Caleb McLaughlin). As he cycles home, he meets the mysterious creature, which has escaped the lab and is on the hunt for prey.

Cut to *Stranger Things*' most sympathetic adults, Will's mother Joyce (Winona Ryder) and police chief Jim Hopper (David Harbour). As Joyce begs Jim to search for her missing son, we begin to learn more about the characters' circumstances: both have suffered serious trauma in their pasts, snippets of which are hinted at in this opening episode.

Back in the forbidding government lab, its intimidating director Dr Martin Brenner (Matthew Modine) has

**Left:** Before the beast came: Will Byers goes about his day, unaware of the events that are about to overtake him.

**Above:** The gang face their deepest fears in night-time Hawkins, Indiana: (from left) Lucas, Mike, Eleven and Dustin.

discovered some strange-looking goop oozing out of the basement, and as we know from all classic Eighties horror, it's never a good idea to go down to the basement. Still, he has other things on his mind, not least the fact that a girl – as yet unidentified – has managed to escape the lab. Grimly, he orders her pursuit.

The runaway kid herself, wearing a hospital gown and a terrified expression, enters a diner, where the owner Benny finds a tattoo on her arm that reads '011'. Eleven, played by Millie Bobby Brown, is all set to be rescued by social services and head off to a happy life when agents sent by Dr Brenner – who has tapped the local phone lines – burst in and kill poor Benny. Using telekinesis, Eleven evades their clutches and escapes into the woods, where she is discovered by Mike, Dustin and Lucas.

Meanwhile, Joyce's landline rings. She picks up, only to hear garbled noises that she thinks might be coming from her missing son. Is it really Will, and if so, where the heck is he calling from?

## CHAPTER TWO:
## THE WEIRDO ON MAPLE STREET

What happens when you come across a homeless waif in the woods? If you're kind-hearted souls like Mike, Dustin and Lucas, you bring her home, sneak her into your room and set her up with a comfy den to sleep in while you debate what on earth to do with her. Mike suggests that they confide in his mum, but Eleven is vehemently against this, warning that 'bad men' are trying to find her – as indeed they are. We don't want that to happen, spooked as we are by what happened to Benny and unnerved by the evil Dr Brenner.

It's time to meet some new characters, the first of which is Will's brother Jonathan (Charlie Heaton), an intense but sweet-natured kid who refuses to give up on his missing sibling. He asks his dad Lonnie (Ross Partridge) for help, but – classic absent father that he is – Lonnie is no use. We're also introduced to Mike's sister Nancy (Natalia Dyer) and her friend Barbara 'Barb' Holland (Shannon Purser), the first of which is accompanied by a jock boyfriend, Steve Harrington (Joe Keery).

Meanwhile, the search for Eleven intensifies, with Hopper's search party finding a bit of her hospital gown near the laboratory she escaped from, raising Hopper's suspicions. Eleven herself helps the boys out with their search for Will, blowing their minds with a demonstration of her telekinetic powers: a key moment in this episode comes when she uses their Dungeons & Dragons board to tell them that Will is on the 'Upside Down' side of the board. Worse, she tells them that he is in danger thanks to the terrible Demogorgon, a Dungeons & Dragons

©Alamy

character whose name they apply to the monster that abducted him.

Just to creep us out even more, when Nancy, Steve and Barb go to a party and Jonathan photographs them in secret, he witnesses Barb sitting by the pool – before she suddenly vanishes, having been attacked by the Demogorgon. Back at Joyce's house, the phone rings, music starts to play on Will's stereo, and the creature itself begins to emerge through the wall. Help!

## CHAPTER THREE: HOLLY, JOLLY

If you thought all that was scary, *Stranger Things* is just getting started. First of all, poor old Barb wakes up, having lost consciousness while being kidnapped by the pool – and who can blame her? Unfortunately, much as we're rooting for her to wake up in her own bed, there's no such luck for Barb – because she's in the Upside Down.

It's hard to explain what the Upside Down is, except to say that it's some sort of parallel dimension that you never, ever want to visit. A cross between the xenomorphs' terrifying hive in *Aliens* and the lonely, windswept heath in *Macbeth* where those horrible witches hang out, the Upside Down is less of a destination and more of a hallucination. Sadly, there's no escape for Barb, who is stalked by the Upside Down's resident monster, the Demogorgon.

Meanwhile, back in the real world, Joyce is out of her mind – or is she? – with grief for her missing son Will, having started to believe that he's communicating with her via lightbulb fluctuations in her home. Meanwhile, Hopper has scheduled a meeting with the wholly untrustworthy Dr Brenner, who shows him fake security footage from the time when Will vanished.

Diligent police officer that he is, Hopper isn't buying any of this, and does a bit of investigation. He unearths Brenner's connection to a previous CIA experiment called Project MKUltra that involved brainwashing subjects with drugs, and also an accusation that Brenner had kidnapped a young girl. In a related scene, Eleven reveals that Brenner was indeed her jailer, and that he once punished her when she declined to use her powers to harm a cat.

Elsewhere, Nancy narrowly escapes from an encounter with the Demogorgon, and Joyce receives a message from Will via an alphabetic board on her wall that says 'Run!' Just as we relax, safe in the knowledge that Will is alive, his body is pulled from a lake in a quarry.

**Right:** When a kid loses his BMX, you know bad things are happening, even if you're Hopper's less-than-professional search team.

©Alamy

## CHAPTER FOUR: THE BODY

Believe us, you want a mum as cool as Joyce, who refuses to believe that the body found in the lake is actually that of her son Will, despite all evidence being to the contrary. No one else believes her stories of Will communicating with her through lightbulbs, but does that stop her? Heck no.

The plot thickens when Eleven convinces Mike that Will's voice can be heard through his toy walkie-talkie, leading the gang to speculate that they can connect to Will more reliably if they use the amateur radio at their school to talk to him. But how will they make this happen? Never underestimate the power of teenage ingenuity.

Not everyone is having as good a time as they are. Finding a photo of Barb that Jonathan took at the party where she disappeared, Nancy notices a rather unpleasant figure approaching her late friend in the picture. Yes, it's the Demogorgon, which Jonathan has heard about from Joyce – herself informed of the evil beastie's existence

through Will's communications – leading him to realise that his mum has been right all along. Nancy's boyfriend Steve fails to grasp the importance of all of this, of course, and they fall out.

Our man Hopper is starting to get suspicious about more or less everything that is going on – to the extent that he applies a severe beating to the state trooper who found Will in the lake. This approach is crude but effective, leading the trooper to admit that he's been ordered to lie about the discovery of the boy's body. Hopper then sneaks into the morgue where Will is lying in state, and who would have thought it, the body turns out to be a fake. Now we're all hopeful that Will is alive again.

But where is he? Fortunately, Eleven and the boys sneak into their school, fire up the ham radio and tune into Will sending messages to Joyce. At her house, Joyce tears away the wallpaper – and sees Will caught in the eerie netherworld behind it.

**Left:** Get on your bikes and ride: in hot pursuit of the gang's missing friend, Will Byers.

**Above:** You wouldn't like her when she's angry: Eleven focuses her mental powers with destruction in mind.

## CHAPTER FIVE:
## THE FLEA AND THE ACROBAT

Hopper is still snooping around the lab in the wake of his discovery, and finds the same mysterious goo that was concerning Dr Brenner a while back. Unfortunately he is discovered by the guards, who knock him out – proving beyond reasonable doubt that something dodgy is going on.

This being the early Eighties, popular science was something that obsessed all right-thinking teenagers. While racking their brains about the possibility of Will communicating with Joyce from an alternate dimension, the boys quiz their friendly science teacher Mr Clarke about the idea of crossing from one dimension to another. He raises the idea that a gate between these different universes might well exist, with the kids realising that such a gate might well mess with the electromagnetic field of Earth. In that case, what better tool than a magnetic compass, every boy scout's favourite accessory?

# "It's hard to explain what the Upside Down is, except to say that it's some sort of parallel dimension that you never, ever want to visit"

**Above:** Who needs school when there's a supernatural monster to track down? Mike and Lucas crack the books.

**Right:** Joyce Byers is the mum everybody wants to have their back: she'll stop at nothing to protect her boys.

Meanwhile, Hopper suddenly wakes up, back at his house. He experiences a Eureka moment when he comes across a hidden microphone and realises that pretty much everything he thought was right was wrong. He's now fully on board with Joyce and her insistence that Will is still around somewhere, even if that somewhere isn't in our dimension.

Talking of which, the gang have been following their compasses around the local countryside in an attempt to locate the gate that will allow them to rescue Will. There's a problem with this plan, though, because Eleven fears that the success of their search will mean she has to encounter the Demogorgon. We learn more about this awful creature in a flashback, when Eleven's memories reveal that she went toe-to-toe with the horrid thing while undergoing one of Brenner's misguided experiments. Trying to avoid this, she messes telekinetically with the

boys' compasses. This annoys Lucas, who fights Mike, although Eleven uses mind control to pull them apart, and runs off.

Nancy and Jonathan are also trying to track down the Demogorgon, with rather more success. While searching in the forest, they come across a deer, which they follow through a gate that leads – you guessed it – to the Upside Down. Uh-oh.

## CHAPTER SIX: THE MONSTER

It's time to discover the link between Eleven and the deadly Demogorgon, and in this episode, that finally happens.

Fortunately for Nancy, she doesn't end up as the Demogorgon's dinner, being pulled out of the Upside Down by Jonathan before the creature can grab her. Thoroughly spooked by the experience, she doesn't want to sleep alone that night, and asks Jonathan if he'll stay in her room overnight. You can't exactly blame her: if you or I had been through this experience, we'd be on the next flight out of Indiana.

Unfortunately, Steve the idiot boyfriend – who is keen to make up with her after their row a while back – sees

© Alamy

her and Jonathan through her bedroom window and totally misinterprets the situation, with the two teenage boys ending up having a good old-fashioned fist-fight. Afterwards, Nancy and Jonathan gather weapons with which to combat the Demogorgon, speculating that the beast is attracted by blood.

Remember when the spooky Dr Brenner was accused of kidnapping someone's daughter? That someone turns out to be a woman called Terry Ives, who is comatose and being looked after by her sister Becky. Joyce and Hopper visit Terry, and Becky explains that her sister had been a participant in Project MKUltra, not knowing that she was pregnant at the time. Becky believes that Terry's baby, a girl named Jane, was kidnapped by Brenner at birth, the evil doctor planning to exploit Jane's remarkable mental powers.

We switch to Eleven, who confirms Becky's story – and her own true identity as Jane Ives – after stealing a ton of snacks from a grocery store. Hey, even masters of telekinesis have to eat. While trying to find her, Mike and Dustin are faced with a gang of bullies who are keen to gain revenge after a previous humiliation at

Eleven's hands. Eleven rescues them, breaking one thug's arm with a satisfying crunch in doing so.

It's time for a full confession, and back at Mike's house, Eleven finally explains to the boys that she has some serious history with the Demogorgon. While trapped by Dr Brenner at the lab, she was obliged to make contact with the monster for reasons best known to the good doctor: in doing so, she accidentally opened the gate to the Upside Down, allowing the Demogorgon to enter our dimension and start killing people. What's saddest about this is that Eleven, or rather Jane, feels that it's all her fault.

As she talks, Brenner's agents surround Mike's house...

## CHAPTER SEVEN: THE BATHTUB

In a tight spot, Mike, Dustin and Eleven run away from the house. The agents pursue them, but Eleven takes care of this by flipping one of their vehicles over. This blocks the pursuers' path, and the kids are safe. For now.

By now, the truth of the whole supernatural situation has become apparent to everybody. Nancy and Jonathan explain that they know about the Demogorgon to Joyce and Hopper, and in a meeting of everyone that we now know and love, they gather to discuss plans. Realising at last that Eleven is actually Jane Ives, the gang asks her to use her telepathy to search for Will and Barb, both of who they hope to be alive in the Upside Down.

But it's not quite as simple as that, unfortunately. Eleven doesn't have infinite sources of energy, and is severely weakened by her defence of the group against the agents. The boys agree that to boost her powers, they will need to find a solution. Science comes to their rescue once again as they break into school and assemble a structure similar to a sensory-deprivation tank, in which Eleven can recuperate, ready to focus her powers once more on finding their lost friends.

Once her energy is restored, Eleven locates Barb in the Upside Down. Hearts broke across a viewing audience of millions when it was revealed that Barb has died, but this was a necessary plot development: how else would we feel that the Demogorgon is really dangerous, and that it must be defeated at all costs?

Eleven also finds Will, who – to our relief – is alive, although he's clinging on for dear life, hiding in the Upside Down equivalent of the fort that he built in their back yard. The question now is how to rescue him. Fortunately, the gang quickly deduces that the gate which gives access to that dimension must be in the basement of Dr Brenner's lab. Hopper and Joyce duly break into the facility, but are arrested by security guards.

Is it game over? Not yet, as Nancy and Jonathan have a cunning plan. They'd better execute it quickly though, because in the Upside Down, the Demogorgon has located Will's fort and is starting to break in.

## CHAPTER EIGHT: THE UPSIDE DOWN

Our terrifying tale draws to a close – for now – but perhaps not in the way we expect. Our hero Hopper, conflicted and haunted by the death of his daughter many years before, has always been a complex character, and he demonstrates this by revealing Eleven's location to Dr Brenner. In return, Brenner allows him and Joyce to enter the Upside Down to attempt to rescue Will.

In a parallel scene, Nancy and Jonathan are planning to attract the monster themselves by cutting their hands, as it loves the scent of blood. The monster appears as soon as the claret starts to flow, as does Nancy's former beau Steve, who intends to apologise for fighting Jonathan. There's no time for apologies, though, as the three youths launch into

combat against the dreaded Demogorgon, managing to set the monster on fire.

Brenner and his goons burst into the school where Eleven and the boys are hiding, but his plans are somewhat thwarted when she uses her powers to wipe out most of his agents – clearly the sensory-deprivation tank was a splendid idea. Brenner's day is spoiled even more when the Demogorgon suddenly appears and kills him. With one last blast of telekinetic energy, Eleven blows the creature to smithereens, but apparently at the cost of her own life, as she disappears with it.

In the Upside Down, Hopper and Joyce find Will: he may have avoided the Demogorgon, but he's been left with a strange tentacle down his throat. They revive him and bring him back to the real world, where he recovers in hospital.

So everything is fine in the end, it seems. A month later, Will vomits up a repulsive slug-like organism, but that can't be significant… can it?

**Below:** Eleven's arrival in the lives of the gang has an impact on each of the members.

**Right:** Dr Brenner presents a civilised front, but in reality he is the cause of the majority of Eleven's problems.

# Season Two 2

## THE PLOT THICKENS AS WE HEAD INTO SEASON 2 OF STRANGER THINGS. WILL WE SURVIVE THE UPSIDE DOWN A SECOND TIME?

WORDS **JOEL MCIVER**

**A**fter a debut season as successful as that of *Stranger Things*, the show was poised to take the world by storm in 2017 – and so it did, breaking records and becoming the most popular streamed original programme on the planet. Audiences and critics alike lined up to heap praise on the development of the story, which amped up the fear of the original run and expanded its universe with cool new characters.

What was most noticeable about season two was its ambition: having set the scene so successfully, the Duffer brothers could have rested on their laurels and essentially repeated themselves, had they so chosen. Not a bit of it: they considered how the *Stranger Things* world could grow, planned trajectories for the characters and made them interact in ways that we hadn't considered.

We get to learn a lot more about a particular central character who we thought was no longer with us (any guesses?) and of course, we're forced to deal with a terrific new monster – although 'terrifying' might be a more appropriate adjective, now we come to think of it.

© Alamy

## CHAPTER ONE: MADMAX

Given the nightmarish nature of the terrifying events of the previous year, by the fall of 1984 the residents of Hawkins, Indiana, are still struggling to come to terms with their encounter with the Demogorgon. In particular, Mike Wheeler and his sister Nancy are grieving for the tragic losses of Eleven and Barb. Still, life can and must go on, with the old gang – Mike, his returned brother Will, Dustin and Lucas – returning to school and being captivated by a new arrival, Maxine 'Max' Mayfield (Sadie Sink).

It's Halloween, and while the town prepares for the coolest night of the year, there's less comfortable stuff going on in Pittsburgh, Pennsylvania. A bank robbery is underway, led by a girl with interesting psychic powers – and a tattoo on her arm that reads 008. Does anything sound familiar about this?

Meanwhile, Joyce Byers is in a new relationship with her old school chum, Bob Newby (Sean Astin), and Hopper is still investigating odd occurrences around the town, namely a field of rotting pumpkins. A new character called Murray Bauman (Brett Gelman), a conspiracy theorist, has heard rumours about what happened in Hawkins the previous year, and is hunting for evidence that might back up his classic Eighties-era theory – that Eleven was a spy sent by the Russians to undermine life in good ol' America.

When season one ended, Will Byers coughed up a repulsive slug of some sort, implying that his travails aren't quite over yet, and indeed he starts our new season hallucinating about a massive monster with tentacles – like the Demogorgon, but even worse, if you can imagine it. Joyce and Hopper speculate that Will is experiencing post-traumatic stress disorder, and take him – guess where? – back to the government lab where it all started.

Yes, this sounds illogical, not to say suicidal, especially as we learn that the gate to the Upside Down in the basement is not only still there, it's expanding, much to the concern of the lab's new boss, Dr Sam Owens. Sci-fi fans will be unnerved to see that Owens is played by Paul Reiser, who was also the villainous Carter Burke in *Aliens*, but the good doctor appears to be a decent chap, so we can relax.

Nancy and her returned boyfriend Steve go and have dinner with Barb's parents, who are convinced that their daughter is alive. So sure are they that they've hired the aforementioned conspiracy nut Murray to search for her.

So all is far from tranquil in Hawkins, Indiana, it seems – but a bigger shock awaits us. Returning to the cabin in the woods where he now lives, Hopper reveals that he has a new housemate: a teenage girl whose hair has now grown out a little and whose name is Eleven. Yes, we punched the air when we saw her – and you did too.

## CHAPTER TWO: TRICK OR TREAT, FREAK

Fortunately, we're given some explanation for Eleven's reappearance: flashbacks show us that she survived the death of the Demogorgon, escaping from the Upside Down and then being pursued by a gang of agents. Hopper provided her with sanctuary, but she's not quite ready to go 'full recluse' just yet, and wants to go trick or treating with her buddies. Sensibly, Hopper refuses, as he's brokering a deal with Dr Owens that will allow her to return to society. In any case, he has other things to worry about, such as a whole town full of rotten pumpkins – caused, he discovers, by the same sticky goo that he once found at the lab.

Elsewhere, Nancy and Steve are arguing again. She wants to 'fess up to Barb's parents about what really happened to their daughter, but Steve – reasonably enough – feels that this would be a bad idea. At a Halloween party, she has one too many cocktails and yells at him for being unsympathetic. Those two, eh?

Meanwhile, Will's hallucinations are getting worse, and he confides in Mike. The two discuss the situation, and Mike reveals that he's been trying to contact Eleven. At the same time, Eleven is trying to establish communications with Mike, with no luck.

We end the episode with an unpleasant surprise for Dustin, who returns home from trick-or-treating to find a strange-looking creature in his dustbin. This can't bode well.

## CHAPTER THREE: THE POLLYWOG

Joyce's boyfriend Bob is a nice guy, and wants Will to get better, so he urges the lad to face up to his fears – although we can safely assume that Bob doesn't know that Will isn't

**Top:** Back in action after we all thought she was Demogorgon fodder, Eleven is tougher than ever in season two.

**Right:** Hopper is back to being a hero – although this time he is the one who ends up needing rescuing.

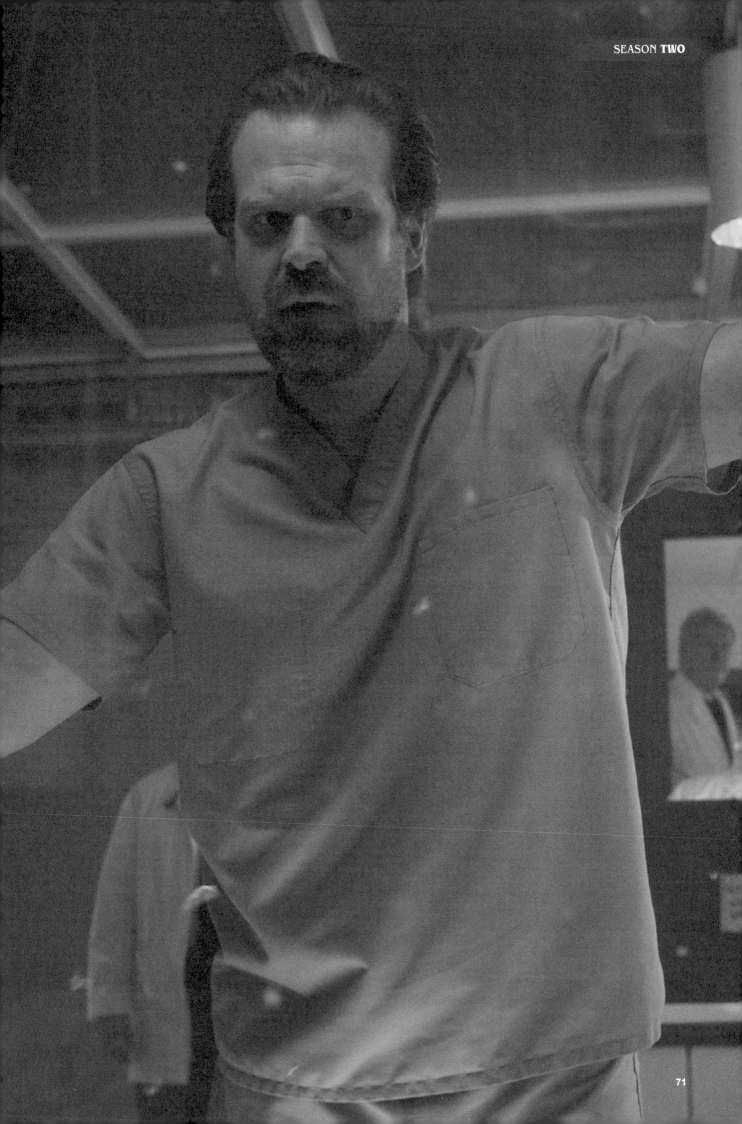

just scared of the dark, he's actually in mortal terror of a giant slavering demon.

More bad advice in this episode comes from Nancy, who persuades Jonathan that it would be an outstanding idea if they told Barb's parents the truth about what happened to their daughter: they arrange to meet them the following day, worrying that Owens might be tapping the phones, as his late predecessor Brenner did. Owens himself is in trouble with Hopper, who thinks that the lab is responsible for the sludge that is destroying the local pumpkins.

Dustin's little buddy from the trashcan resembles a slug of some kind: apparently not spooked by the arrival of yet another creepy organism, he nicknames it D'Artagnan ('Dart') and takes it to meet his buddies. They conclude that it's from the Upside Down, as Will recognises the noise it makes from his ongoing hallucinations. Why they don't stamp on it immediately is not made clear.

Bored of being stuck in Hopper's cabin in the woods, Eleven sneaks out and goes to see Mike. Seeing him chatting with new girl Max at the school, she assumes the two are flirting and leaves, saddened by what she has witnessed. The love-story subplot and the horror plotline are weaving neatly in and out of each other at this point: nice writing, Duffer brothers.

During another terrifying hallucination about the tentacled monster, Will heeds Bob's friendly if ill-advised tips and goes toe-to-toe with the beast. This doesn't work out in his favour, as it grabs him and jams one of its tendrils down his throat. You'd think the poor kid would have suffered enough by now...

## CHAPTER FOUR: WILL THE WISE

Fortunately, Will is revived by Joyce and his buddies, and is apparently well enough to go home – although when he gets there, he starts exhibiting some bizarre behaviour, drawing weird designs on paper and asking that the house be kept at an ice-cold temperature. Hopper comes over to investigate, and together they figure out that his drawings line up to represent vine-like plants.

We're given much more of an insight into the character of Dr Owens in this episode. His goons grab Nancy and Jonathan when they try to connect with Barb's mother, and take them to the government lab. Here, Owens comes clean about the gate to the Upside Down, which now looks even less welcoming than it did

**Right:** Kids today, eh? You don't know if they're cleaning up the streets or chasing down a monster from another world.

**Above:** Lucas Sinclair and the girl that the whole school is talking about, Max Mayfield: crazy older brother not pictured.

**Right:** Nancy and Jonathan are grabbed by Dr Owens and his goons as they try to reach out to Barb's mother.

# "Seeing Mike chatting with new girl Max at school, Eleven assumes the two are flirting and leaves, saddened by what she has witnessed"

before, and admits that Barb died in there. However, he wants to keep foreign governments from finding out about it – probably wisely, given the circumstances. Once Nancy and Jonathan are allowed to leave, the former reveals that she caught all of Owens' confession on tape – a resourceful move.

It all goes badly pear-shaped at this point, with Lucas trying to get friendly with Max, only to be prevented from doing so by her psychopathic big brother, Billy Hargrove (Dacre Montgomery). Eleven and Hopper have a massive row about her leaving his cabin, which ends when she blows out the windows in telekinetic anger. Cleaning up the broken glass the next day, she discovers evidence that Terry Ives is her biological mother, and attempts to contact her using her mind powers.

The bad news we were all expecting comes when Dustin discovers that his pet slug Dart has escaped its cage, breakfasted on the family cat and evolved into a baby Demogorgon. He can't say he wasn't warned, can he? It all

gets even worse when Hopper, digging up some decaying pumpkins, discovers a tunnel that leads directly to the Upside Down.

## CHAPTER FIVE: DIG DUG

"Wait! Don't go down there!" we all shout at the screen as Hopper enters the dread tunnel to the Upside Down, and we're absolutely right to do so, because he soon gets stuck and faints. Fortunately for him, Will experiences a vision that reveals Hopper's whereabouts, assisted by Joyce's boyfriend Bob, who interprets Will's hallucination and identifies the pumpkin field where the over-enthusiastic police officer was last seen.

We now get to spend some time with the keen conspiracy theorist Murray, who listens to the tape of Owens' confessions made by Nancy. He correctly thinks that no one will believe any of it, but that perhaps an edited version of events might encourage people to investigate. In fact, it's fessing-up time all round, as the lovelorn Lucas

reveals all about what happened to Will to his crush, Max. Meanwhile, the gang are trying to catch Dart, trapping the newborn monster in Dustin's basement – but remember, in *Stranger Things*, things never work out well in basements.

Back to Eleven, who finds out where her mother Terry and her aunt Becky live, and heads over for a visit. Terry, still comatose, can be reached successfully via telekinesis, and she and her long-lost daughter communicate. Eleven learns that her mother tried to rescue her from the clutches of the evil Dr Brenner, but he zapped Terry with enough shock therapy to damage her brain, hence her current state of catatonia. Terry also informs her that there was another girl at the lab who had psychic powers, too.

Finally, Hopper is pulled out from the tunnel to the Upside Down by Joyce, Bob, Will and Mike. Lab scientists then set the tunnels on fire for reasons best known to themselves – and the moment this happens, Will collapses to the ground in terrible pain.

## CHAPTER SIX: THE SPY

Will is in a bad way, with his memory gone and his body apparently being controlled by some invisible force. After he's taken to the lab, Owens steps up to help, speculating that the tentacled monster of Will's hallucinations has spread like a virus into his brain. This will explain why the fire in the tunnels was so painful to Will.

Fortunately, more positive events are taking place elsewhere. Nancy and Jonathan enter into a romantic relationship, encouraged by Murray, who persuades them to admit their true feelings, and they send copies of the tape containing Owens' supernatural tale to newspapers around the United States.

Elsewhere, Lucas and Max join Dustin and Steve on a mission to catch Dart in an old junkyard. When their once-friendly, now-lethal slug buddy arrives, the gang see to their horror that it is accompanied by a load of half-grown monsters of the Upside Down persuasion – and while they may be adolescents rather than the fully adult and fully terrifying creatures we've met before, they're still scary. However, just as the pack of monsters is about to turn the gang of unfortunate teenagers into brunch, they suddenly change their minds and run away.

In the meantime, Owens has been considering a plan of action. Will mentions an area that he can't see, blocked off by the king monster that is controlling him, so Owens

sends a team to search for it – not realising that this is what It wants all along. His team is duly overrun by the half-sized monsters, who then penetrate the lab and begin stalking their human adversaries.

## CHAPTER SEVEN: THE LOST SISTER

While our heroes await their fate in the lab at the hands of a cohort of monsters from the Upside Down, the action shifts to Chicago, where Eleven goes to track down the girl that her mother Terry had mentioned in their earlier telepathic chat. The girl (Linnea Berthelsen), who bears the '008' tattoo that we encountered back in episode one of this season, is called Kali: the two soon bond after realising that they were both experimented upon by Dr Brenner.

Like Eleven, Kali – or Eight, if you prefer – has led a troubled life. In Chicago, she is the leader of a street gang, and has the psychic ability to broadcast images into people's minds. She teaches Eleven that her own powers will be maximised if she learns to channel her anger. Kali's goal, to seek revenge against Brenner, is proven useless when Eleven tells her that her target is dead, so she switches her desire for revenge to Ray, the man who tortured Terry Ives.

On finding Ray at his apartment, Eleven uses her powers to choke him; as he struggles, he swears that Dr Brenner is still alive. Noticing a picture of Ray's two young daughters,

she refuses to kill him, and prevents Kali from doing the same. Returning to the gang's hideout, Kali tells Eleven that she must either stay in Chicago and avenge her mother, or go back to Indiana. Eleven's decision is made for her when she suddenly experiences a vision of Mike and the Hawkins gang, trapped in Dr Owens' lab and facing down a swarm of murderous creatures.

As Kali and her gang escape from the local cops, Eleven heads for home – but will she get there in time?

## CHAPTER EIGHT: THE MIND FLAYER

All bets are off back at the lab in Hawkins. The adolescent monsters may not be as dangerous as their full-grown counterparts, but they're still plenty threatening, storming the lab and wiping out the staff. What on earth are Mike, Joyce, Hopper, Bob, Dr Owens and the unconscious Will to do?

Well, if we've learned anything from *Stranger Things*, it's that these resourceful people tend to come up with good ideas in a tight spot. While the carnage unfolds around them, they come up with the idea that Will is essentially functioning as an involuntary spy for the boss monster in the Upside Down: Mike persuades Joyce to give Will a sedative, in doing so hiding their location. Once Will is out cold, they take him to the lab's security zone to make a last stand against the invading horde.

**Left:** Karen Wheeler (Cara Buono), mother of Nancy and Mike, is blissfully unaware of what her kids are up to.

**Above:** The icing on the cake of the season two finale: Eleven is allowed to attend the Snow Ball like a normal kid.

Unfortunately, the power goes down. How will they reset it? With a brave volunteer, in this case Bob, who sets out to reset the breakers at the power terminal. Against the odds, the resourceful fellow makes his way there and switches the power back on: this allows Mike, Joyce, Hopper and Will to escape, with Owens staying behind to guide Bob out when he gets back from his mission. Sadly for Bob, he is promptly murdered by the creatures right in front of Joyce.

The gang now reunites with Nancy, Jonathan, Steve, Dustin, Lucas and Max – in fact, more or less everybody in the series – at the Byers house, where they take a moment in order to assess the situation. Once again, Dungeons & Dragons helps to add some clarity to the proceedings, with Dustin naming the monster that controls Will the 'Mind Flayer' after a character from the game. They realise that killing it is the only option, but if they do so while it still infects Will, they'll kill him too. They manage to communicate with the comatose Will using Morse code, who instructs them to close the gate in the lab.

While they're pondering this, the Mind Flayer's creatures close in on the house: one crashes through the window, but it's dead. Who should walk in but Eleven, who has killed the rest of the monsters. Rarely has any character been as welcome.

## CHAPTER NINE: THE GATE

With the key characters reunited, all that remains now is to kill the Mind Flayer without also killing Will, close the gate to the Upside Down, and save the entire world from being invaded by ghoulish monsters. No problem for any early Eighties pack of teenagers, you'll agree.

The plan that they cook up is as follows. First, Hopper and Eleven head to the lab to close the gate. On arrival, they meet Dr Owens, who everyone thought had died right after Bob, but got away with a few injuries. At the same time, Jonathan, Nancy and Joyce overheat Will: you'll recall that he insisted that he remain cold in the early stage of the Mind Flayer's control. Being jabbed with a red-hot poker does the trick, purging the virus from Will and leaving the rest of the gang free to kick some Flayer butt.

Next, Mike, Dustin, Lucas, Max and Steve set up a decoy movement, heading into the burned-out tunnels in an attempt to lure the pack of monsters away from the lab where Hopper and Eleven are headed. A brief distraction by Max's brother Billy, who gets into a fight with Steve, is quickly resolved, and it's game on.

Finally, Eleven and the Mind Flayer face off. It's something of a David versus Goliath situation, with the monster towering above our heroine, but she channels her anger, killing its flocks of monster soldiers and closing the gate. We breathe a sigh of relief.

Jumping forward a month, the lab has closed thanks to the newspapers who ran stories based on Nancy's tape, Barb is given a funeral, and Dr Owens fakes a birth certificate for Eleven, renaming her Jane Hopper. The kids duly attend a winter shindig at school, and it all seems pretty tranquil until we suddenly switch to the Upside Down, where the huge Mind Flayer is standing over the school, watching the kids having fun, and biding its time...

**Right:** Eleven further hones her abilities when she meets fellow lab subject Kali, aka 'Eight', in Chicago.

# Season Three 3

### IF YOU THOUGHT THINGS IN HAWKINS WERE WEIRD BEFORE, THEY'RE ONLY JUST GETTING STARTED...

WORDS **JOEL MCIVER**

First broadcast in July 2019, the third season of *Stranger Things* had one simple mission: to extend, expand and improve upon its solid-gold first two seasons. That might sound simple to you and me, but when it comes to determining the direction of a fictional universe that has gained the love and respect of literally millions of fans worldwide, finding the right way forward is a bit like entering a gate into the Upside Down itself – fraught with missteps and easy to mess up.

Fortunately, the Duffer brothers, their cast and their crew pulled off a truly spectacular feat. Developing characters we already loved, introducing highly watchable new folks and getting them into seemingly impossible scrapes, the *Stranger Things* creative team wrote and produced arguably their most compelling season yet. Critics loved it; over 64 million households tuned into the first month of shows; and the cast became bona fide stars. However they're doing it over at *ST* HQ, they're doing it brilliantly – so let's see how it all went down!

© Alamy

## CHAPTER ONE: SUZIE, DO YOU COPY?

We open our third journey into the unsettling world of Hawkins, Indiana, with a brief flashback to June 1984, a few months before the harrowing events of season two. Who's this trying to break into the Upside Down? Why, it's a team of military scientists from the Soviet Union, America's avowed enemy at this period in history – and we have a real bad feeling about this.

Jump forward a year to the summer of 1985, and it doesn't seem that Live Aid and the release of Megadeth's debut album has left a smile on the faces of anyone in Hawkins. Instead, there's a new shopping mall called Starcourt, which is so popular that a bunch of local businesses have been forced to shut down, annoying the residents.

How is the gang doing after the last couple of years of trauma? Well, Mike and Eleven are in a relationship, although Jim Hopper – now the latter's legal dad – isn't best pleased about this. Dustin has a girlfriend, Suzie (Gabriella Pizzolo), and is using a homemade radio pylon to communicate with her: in doing so, he picks up a garbled message in the Russian language. As for Will, he's generally troubled, fearing – accurately, as we know – that the terrible Mind Flayer is actually alive and well and about to cause problems again.

Do you remember Billy Hargrove, Max's older brother? You'll recall that in season two, he was keenly interested in hitting people. In season three, it turns out that he's also interested in hitting *on* people, namely Mike and Nancy's mother Karen. And, on the way to visit her for a "meeting of minds", he's ambushed by some form of unseen monster and dragged into a nearby mill. We already know that this is an undesirable outcome because a few minutes ago, we saw a flock of rats run into this mill and explode messily, congealing into an unsavoury lump of flesh and goo.

So it's business as usual in Hawkins. What are the Soviets up to? What's going to happen to Billy? And what's the significance of Starcourt Mall? All will be revealed, but it won't be pleasant.

## CHAPTER TWO: THE MALL RATS

Billy isn't having a great time in the rat-infested mill, it has to be said. The spooky, animated blob, made up of ex-rats, causes him to enter a hallucination in which he sees the Upside Down in all its horrible glory. Here, he meets his own doppelgänger and is tortured with strange visions and creepy voices. Possessed, he comes out of his trance and heads off on a mission: the unpleasant creature has convinced him to go to the swimming pool where he works as a lifeguard, kidnap his colleague, Heather Holloway (Francesca Reale), and bring her to the mill.

**Top:** Billy Hargrove, soon to be possessed by the Mind Flayer, makes a move on the equally enamoured Karen Wheeler.

**Right:** Hawkins' highly dodgy mayor, Larry Kline. Would you trust a man with that much self-assurance?

Meanwhile, Nancy and Jonathan are working as interns at the local newspaper, the *Hawkins Post*. They're sent to interview an elderly local, Mrs Driscoll (Peggy Miley), who has reported that psychotic rats are eating her garden fertiliser. While they're poking around, they fail to witness a rat repeating the trick we saw at the old mill by exploding into a nasty lump of meat.

We check in briefly with the series' ongoing romantic subplot, and witness Eleven breaking up with Mike because he lied to her in order to avoid seeing her. In his defence, he did this because Hopper forced him to do so, over-worrying dad that he is. Other developments in Hawkins this week include Joyce Byers' discovery that magnetic items at home and work don't seem to be magnetic any more, a pain for any fridge-magnet collector.

We end with Dustin, Nancy's former beau Steve and a colleague called Robin Buckley (Maya 'Uma Thurman's daughter' Hawke) – who works at Starcourt Mall's ice-cream parlour with Steve – trying to figure out the Russian-language message that Dustin received while chatting to Suzie. Due to the Russian language not being commonly taught in Indiana high schools at this point in sociopolitical history, none of them understand it. They do figure out that it must be a code of some kind, but a code for what?

## CHAPTER THREE: THE CASE OF THE MISSING LIFEGUARD

Everything escalates at an alarming pace in this episode, with plot reveals aplenty. We begin with Eleven, now boyfriend-free, who uses her telekinetic powers to see what her ex-chap Mike is up to. He isn't doing much, so she switches focus to Billy, who – as a violent sociopath possessed by the Upside Down – is a more interesting subject. His sister Max has recently discovered that he's missing, so it's a relief for her when he shows up on Eleven's mental sat-nav, but unfortunately Billy's newly acquired possession allows him to sense that Eleven is watching him. Uh-oh...

She isn't the only person finding things out in Hawkins this week. Nancy and Jonathan, the intrepid journalists, are now hearing multiple reports of garden fertiliser being stolen from households and rats behaving oddly. Visiting Mrs Driscoll again, they witness the senior citizen munching on some fertiliser herself, a disturbing development by anyone's standards.

**Right:** It's not all doom and gloom for Eleven: at heart, she's a kid like any other, who would enjoy life if the adults let her.

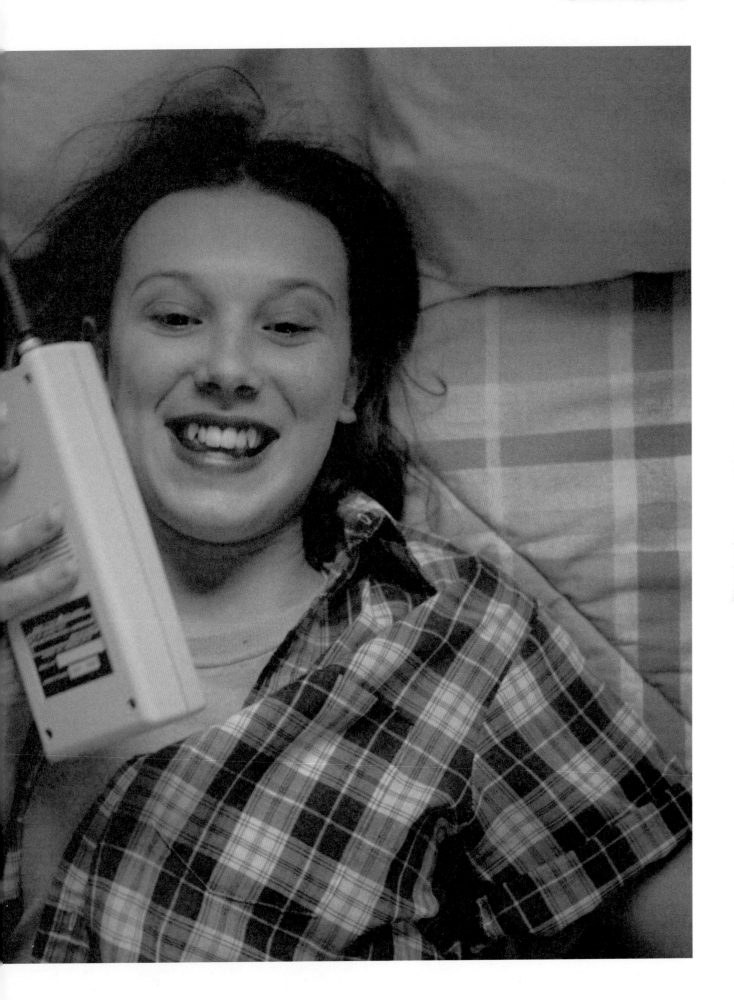

# "Will Byers senses from afar that the dreaded Mind Flayer is back – and is, disturbingly, as actively malevolent as ever!"

**Below:** Billy finally sees the light and sacrifices himself for the greater good in the season finale.

**Right:** Strange things are afoot in Hawkins, Indiana, with Eleven (far right) in command of terrifying mental powers.

The 'evil Russians' trope of so much Eighties sci-fi is now fully up and running, with Robin decoding the mysterious transmission and revealing that a shipment from the Soviet Union is about to arrive at Starcourt Mall that evening; later, she, Steve and Dustin witness a posse of gun-toting Russian military arriving with said shipment in tow.

The Russians aren't only at the mall, it transpires. Joyce, who is unduly worried by the lack of magnetism that she's discovered, speculates that the demagnetisation might come from the now-abandoned lab run until recently by Doctors Brenner and Owens. Heading over to the old place, the duo of Joyce and Hopper encounter a Russian soldier called Grigori (Andrey Ivchenko), who attacks Hopper.

Billy, who is mentally enslaved by the Upside Down, and his workmate Heather, who has also fallen under the spell

of the unpleasant rat-creature, are apparently recruiting for the occult cause. They visit Heather's parents, where Max and Eleven drop in to meet them; after those two leave, Billy and Heather subdue poor old Mom and Dad.

From afar, Will Byers senses that this has happened, realising, to his horror, that this is the dreaded work of the Mind Flayer, who is as actively malevolent as ever.

## CHAPTER FOUR: THE SAUNA TEST

The evil mill is now the centre of operations for the Mind Flayer, who has taken on a physical form, if an unpleasant one – it's made up of flesh from all the exploded rats. Billy and Heather bring the latter's parents to it, where it possesses them, bringing its army of controlled humans to four. This doesn't bode well.

Escaping from their encounter with Grigori, Hopper and Joyce visit the mayor of Hawkins, Larry Kline (Carey Elwes of *Saw* and *The Princess Bride*), based on Hopper's recollection that he once saw Kline and Grigori together. Under pressure, Kline eventually admits that Starcourt Mall is nothing but a front for the Russians, who are buying up abandoned properties across the town for their own nefarious purposes.

Indeed, Starcourt is becoming less and less welcoming: when Dustin, Steve and Robin – accompanied by Lucas Sinclair's sister Erica (Priah Ferguson) – visit the mall, they discover that the loading dock that leads inside is actually an elevator. It traps them beneath the mall which, while worrying, does at least put them in a position to explore the shady goings-on down there.

And 'shady' is the key adjective here, because the town of Hawkins is now subject to all sorts of strange occurrences. After she and Jonathan are fired by their boss, who happens to be Heather's father, for harassing Mrs Driscoll one too many times, Nancy sneaks over to the hospital where the elderly lady is incarcerated. Before her eyes, Mrs D becomes possessed by the Mind Flayer.

At the same time, Will explains to Mike, Lucas, Eleven, and Max, that he has developed a mental connection to the monster and they agree that Billy's actions can only mean that he is enslaved to the creature. They attempt to trap him in the sauna at the swimming pool to demonstrate this – remember, the Mind Flayer likes the cold – but he breaks out, highly aggrieved and clearly planning to murder the lot of them. Fortunately, Eleven steps in and overpowers him with telekinesis, pinning him down with a barbell.

Later, Billy returns to the mill – where we witness a whole crowd of possessed Hawkins townsfolk. Oh dear…

## CHAPTER FIVE: THE FLAYED

Multiple storylines are now ongoing, with the overall braid – as they call it in the movies – adding up to a thrilling web of supernatural action. In this episode, the primary arc belongs to Hopper and Joyce, who search through one of the abandoned properties mentioned in Kline's confession.

What do they find? A hidden lab belonging to the Soviets! Chased down by the relentless Grigori, they manage to get away, taking a Russian scientist named Alexei (Alec Utgoff) along as hostage. He doesn't speak English, and Hopper and Joyce certainly don't speak Russian, so they take him to Murray Bauman, our old conspiracy-theory buddy, because Murray happens to speak the language.

Meanwhile, Dustin, Steve, Robin and Erica also find a Russian lab, this time underneath Starcourt Mall, where they witness soldiers unloading boxes of some unknown material from the elevator. While searching for a radio room in order to call for help, they stumble across a massive room where Soviet boffins are doing what we thought they were doing this entire time – trying to open a portal to the Upside Down. Could there be a worse idea than that?

In one of their periodic group get-togethers, Nancy, Jonathan, Will, Mike, Lucas, Eleven and Max come up with the idea that Billy and the fertiliser-chomping Mrs Driscoll have been possessed by the Mind Flayer. Once possessed, they're recruiting more people to be 'flayed' – or mentally enslaved – in order to create an army that will battle on behalf of the Upside Down. They're attacked by two of the Flayed, and although Nancy and Jonathan manage to kill them, they turn into a grisly mass that looks like the Mind Flayer itself.

## CHAPTER SIX: E PLURIBUS UNUM

In between all the occult action, Eleven and Mike are undergoing a Ross-and-Rachel-style on-off romance, never quite getting together and never quite parting ways either. You can't help but root for the couple, who deserve a bit of happiness after all they've been through.

Or should we say, 'are going through', because there's no let-up whatsoever in the endless barrage of life-threatening

**Right:** (From left to right) Will, Lucas, Dustin and Max watch as Eleven and Mike saunter off for a pubescent-styled kissing sesh.

© Alamy

occurrences in Hawkins. Things seem to be going well as this episode begins, with Eleven incapacitating the Mind Flayer to the extent that it retreats back to its nest at the old mill. Steve and Robin, who have been caught by the Russians in the lab underneath Starcourt Mall and interrogated, are rescued by Dustin and Erica.

Moreover, Murray's grasp of Russian has come in handy because he's translated the words of Hopper and Joyce's hostage Alexei, who confirms that his Russian colleagues are actively trying to get into the Upside Down via the portal they're constructing beneath Starcourt. Hopper calls our old chum Dr Owens and asks him to warn the government about the clandestine Soviet incursion, although – as all sci-fi fans know – you can never trust the government. We are reminded of this one more time when Hawkins' corrupt mayor Larry Kline is approached by the Soviet agent Grigori, who wants him to find Hopper and hand him over.

It's time to confront the Mind Flayer before it overtakes the entire town and maybe even our entire dimension, so Eleven communicates via telepathy with its prime ambassador Billy. In doing so we learn that the lad had a miserable childhood, and we gain a bit of sympathy for him, but there's little time for kissing and making up because Billy tells the Mind Flayer where Eleven is.

It's apparent that the Mind Flayer wants Eleven dead in revenge for destroying the original gate under the old lab, and in due course a horde of Flayed gather at the mill,

merging with their boss in one giant, monstrous figure. You really wouldn't want to annoy it, but unfortunately, Eleven already has.

## CHAPTER SEVEN: THE BITE

We're heading rapidly towards the most dramatic season conclusion yet, with multiple storylines resolved – or not, as the case may be – and the fates of many much-loved characters in the balance. In this penultimate episode, the gang know that a showdown between the Mind Flayer and Eleven is imminent, and indeed it happens suddenly, leaving our heroine seriously injured and the kids just about escaping the monster before it kills them all.

The Mind Flayer isn't the only adversary, of course, with a whole brigade of Russian scientists and soldiers for the Hawkins residents to deal with – those Hawkins residents who haven't been turned into an army of the practically undead, of course. Dustin, Erica, Steve and Robin take

refuge in the cinema at Starcourt Mall, while Eleven's group just want one thing – to help her recover from the injury she sustained while battling the Mind Flayer. They hole up in a supermarket to gather supplies, where Dustin contacts them over walkie-talkie to inform them of what's going on at the mall. In due course, they all gather at Starcourt, where the final confrontation is set to take place.

It's all looking pretty bleak. Hopper's team search everywhere for the kids, winding up at a fairground where they are seen by the unreliable mayor, Kline. He tells the Russians where they are, and in due course the soldiers track Hopper down. The scientist, Alexei, is shot dead by Grigori, and it looks as if the same fate awaits the rest of them, despite a brilliant diversionary tactic by Murray, who confuses their attackers by speaking Russian to them.

Eleven is in a bad way by now – and although her group arrives at the mall and saves Dustin from being shot by

she uses her powers to blast open her wound and eject the piece of Mind Flayer that was stuck in it. While this is undoubtedly the sensible thing to do, the move also removes her mental powers completely: after this, she can't even crush a can of Coke with telekinesis, let alone take on a skyscraper-sized monster.

So who's going to defeat the Mind Flayer? Read on...

After many manoeuvres, the team find themselves at the gate constructed by the Soviets to the Upside Down. Earlier, Alexei told them how to explode the gate, the building and the Mind Flayer – if only they can do it without blowing themselves up too. Standing between them and victory are Billy and Grigori; although she has no telekinetic powers, Eleven can still communicate telepathically, and she reminds Billy of the childhood love of his mother, which snaps him out of the Mind Flayer's mental control. Apologising to his sister Max for his behaviour, Billy delays the monster's attack by sacrificing himself.

As for Grigori, it's time for Jim Hopper to show his quality: he fights and defeats the *Terminator*-like Russian, but in doing so gets trapped in the very machinery that they're trying to destroy. With no other option, and time running out because the Mind Flayer is preparing to deliver a final blow, he nods to Joyce to destroy the gate. In tears, she complies – and the massive explosion destroys the gate, the soldiers, and apparently Hopper (crushing any hopes fans had for a Jim-Joyce romance). The cavalry arrives in the form of Dr Owens plus American soldiers, as the Mind Flayer dies.

the Russians, her energy is spent and she collapses. We zoom in for a look at the wound she sustained in the fight with the Mind Flayer: there's something very unusual about it.

## CHAPTER EIGHT: THE BATTLE OF STARCOURT

The final episode of season three of *Stranger Things* is an object lesson in how to write a compelling conclusion and wring emotions, good and bad, out of every scene. We really need ten pages to analyse it fully, but let's just say that this excellent chunk of TV revolves around the concept of self-sacrifice for the greater good.

Cleverly, the writers immediately remove any expectations we may have had that this season is going to end with yet another climactic scene of Eleven versus monster, in which she defeats her adversary with her telekinetic strength. Far from it: as the episode opens,

We cut to three months later. Starcourt is no more. The multiple deaths, including those of the Flayed, have been attributed to the mall's destruction. Kline has been disgraced and arrested. The Byers family, with whom the still-powerless Eleven now lives, are on the point of moving to California, and who can blame them? Mike and Eleven finally declare their love for each other and plan to meet at Thanksgiving.

So that's it, then? Everything's all right now?

Come on, you know better than that. This is *Stranger Things*, after all, and in a mid-credits scene we're taken briefly to Kamchatka in Russia. In a grim government facility, guards are ordered to feed a prisoner to a full-sized captive Demogorgon – but "not the American", they're told. Hooper, is that you?

Looks like season four is going to have some surprises...

# Season Four

## PACK YOUR FURRY HAT, KIDS – IN SEASON FOUR, WE'RE GOING ON A RESCUE MISSION TO RUSSIA!

WORDS **JOEL MCIVER**

Season three of *Stranger Things* ended as all its seasons do, with the characters in a state of absolute chaos but with a sense of cosy optimism. After all, they had defeated the unholy might of the Upside Down with nothing but friendship, solidarity and positivity, although Eleven's superpowers admittedly helped them out a lot, too. Still, there was a weird edge of tension to the ending of S3 that needed to be resolved – namely because Eleven and the Byers family were breaking up the Hawkins gang by moving to California, and also because Netflix told us that we're going to Russia.

Why is this? Because that's where Jim Hopper is!

Yes, friends, the biggest question about *Stranger Things'* fourth season was answered a while back: what the heck happened to Hopper? As you know, we saw him vanish in a giant explosion at the end of season three; as you also know, a mid-credits outro scene saw a Russian guard instruct his colleagues not to feed "the American" to their pet Demogorgon.

So, *Stranger Things* goes international in season four, and as it turns out, is responsible for introducing the music of two particularly amazing artists to a new generation. Who would have predicted that?

**Above:** Wait, we thought Dr Brenner was dead? Fortunately, by the end of season four, he absolutely will be.

**Right:** Lucas, Steve and Dustin witness Max being possessed by Vecna at Billy's grave. You'd be freaked out, too.

© Alamy

## CHAPTER ONE: THE HELLFIRE CLUB

We have a couple of parallel storylines going on in our first episode, introduced by a flashback to 1979 when we see Dr Brenner (remember him?) experimenting on a bunch of superpower-endowed kids, at least until they're all wiped out, leaving only Eleven alive. Well, that's a cheerful start.

Back in 1986, we're eight months into life after the Starcourt Mall drama. Joyce, Will, Jonathan and Eleven have moved to California, but it's no fun over in the Golden State, with Eleven now powerless and a victim of bullying by the usual Eighties schoolyard thugs. More cheerfully, Joyce receives a Russian doll in the mail with a note confirming that Hopper is still alive. The power of the postal service, eh?

Back in Hawkins, life goes on more or less as usual, in other words everyone is trying to get through the day without being attacked by demonic forces. Mike and Dustin are playing Dungeons & Dragons with the oddball Eddie Munson, while Max is grieving for Billy. A cheerleader called Chrissy Cunningham is experiencing visions of a creepy humanoid, and after she gets freaked out by dreams of her family and a weird grandfather clock, said humanoid takes control of her mind and kills her. Eddie witnesses this and runs for his life.

Welcome back to *Stranger Things*, people: it's only going to get weirder.

## CHAPTER TWO: VECNA'S CURSE

We switch to Kamchatka, a grim Russian outpost, where the great Hopper is languishing in the prison cell that we glimpsed at the end of season three. He's holding up, just about, having bribed a prison guard called Dmitri Antonov (aka Enzo) to help him break out. Enzo is the fellow who wrote to Joyce, who duly calls him and is told to send a $40,000 ransom to one of his dodgy mates in Alaska. How Joyce is meant to come up with that much cash is evidently not Enzo's problem.

In California, Mike is on a pleasant visit to Eleven, rendered less pleasant when she smacks a school bully in the face with a rollerskate. Over in Hawkins, Max tells Dustin that she saw Eddie heading for the hills on the night that Chrissy was killed by the unknown spooky figure. Robin and Steve help them find Eddie, who is understandably traumatised by what he saw that night. Realising that the murder must be an incursion by the Upside Down, Eddie and Dustin come up with the name Vecna for the homicidal villain, nabbing the name from Dungeons & Dragons (again).

Nancy and her student reporter chum Fred are investigating Chrissy's death too, and meet Eddie's uncle, who points the finger at a deranged fellow called Victor Creel, locked up three decades previously after supposedly killing his family. Afterwards, Fred is lured into the nearby

woods by strange visions, which turns out to be a poor choice because Vecna shows up and kills him.

## CHAPTER THREE: THE MONSTER AND THE SUPERHERO

Our friendly scientist, Dr Sam Owens, takes a meeting with a US army officer, Lieutenant Colonel Jack Sullivan, who thinks that Eleven had a hand in Chrissy's death. Never mind that she was in California at the time, right? Meanwhile, Eleven herself is in a spot of bother on the other side of the country, having been arrested for the rollerskate assault: fortunately, Owens intervenes and she agrees to accompany him back to Hawkins, incentivised no doubt by his promise to help restore her powers.

Joyce and our old friend Murray are doing some travelling of their own, flying to Alaska to deliver $40,000 as a ransom for Hopper, who is making progress over in Kamchatka: he's paid a fellow prisoner to smash his shackles with a sledgehammer.

In Hawkins, it's all kicking off in multiple locations. First, Nancy and Robin discover at the local library (remember those?) that Victor Creel blamed his family's murders on

a demonic creature of some sort, which they immediately connect with Vecna. Then the school basketball team, of which Lucas is now a keen member, go on a hunt for Eddie in a classic jocks-versus-nerds scenario. They think that Eddie must have been responsible for Chrissy's death, but Lucas doesn't buy this and walks away.

Finally, Max finds out that Chrissy visited the school counsellor before her death: stealing Chrissy's files from the office, and those of Nancy's late colleague Fred for good measure, she discovers that both were suffering from PTSD, just as she was herself. The episode closes with Max hallucinating about a grandfather clock and hearing Vecna call her name. Oh dear...

## CHAPTER FOUR: DEAR BILLY

So, all Joyce and Murray have to do is hand over $40,000 to Enzo's Alaskan contact and Hopper will be set free, correct? Wrong. They do meet the contact, Yuri, but he slips them an incapacitating drug, planning to serve them up on a platter alongside Hopper and Enzo to the Russians in return for mucho roubles. The scoundrel! In fact Hopper does manage to escape his captors for a while, but they easily nab him again, so unfortunately it's all back to square one in the Hopper storyline.

Dr Owens has arranged for two of his agents, Wallace and Harmon, to keep an eye on Jonathan, Mike and Will, but the kids aren't having this and plan to escape. Before this can happen, a posse of soldiers attacks their house:

**Left:** The geek shall inherit the earth: misfit Eddie Munson rolls the dice in Dungeons & Dragons.

**Above:** You wouldn't like her when she's angry: Eleven gets her powers back and uses them to full effect.

with the aid of Jonathan's chum Argyle they get away, taking the injured agent Harmon along.

In Hawkins, the imprisoned Victor Creel tells a visiting Nancy and Robin that his family were tortured to death by occult monsters. Elsewhere, Max is possessed by Vecna. She had expected this to happen, given her previous hallucinations, and had gone to Billy's gravestone to read him a farewell letter. Steve, Dustin and Lucas, who witness this, have been told by Nancy and Robin that music can defeat Vecna, so they play 'Running Up That Hill' by Kate Bush at Max. It's her favourite song, as indeed it became the whole world's new favourite song after this episode was broadcast, and it enables Max to break free of Vecna.

## CHAPTER FIVE: THE NINA PROJECT

Owens is now attempting to get Eleven her repressed childhood memories back, a feat that he almost pulls off when he takes her to NINA, an isolation tank in an old nuclear weapons facility in Nevada. Although she tries to escape (there's a lot of escaping this season, isn't there?) the fact that her superpowers briefly return persuades her to give the NINA effort a go.

Other scenarios play out in this episode. Agent Harmon gifts the boys the NINA project's phone number, and they ask Dustin's girlfriend Suzie, who is in Salt Lake City, to help them out. On the plane to Russia, Joyce and Murray manage to incapacitate the evil Yuri: fortunately, they survive the subsequent crash-landing slap bang in the middle of nowhere.

As is so often the case in *Stranger Things*, groups of characters are starting to merge in pursuit of a common goal, and so Max, Lucas, Steve, and Dustin connect with Nancy and Robin and they all head to the spooky old Creel house. Once there, they see a bunch of flickering lights, which they soon deduce can be used to follow Vecna's movements in the Upside Down.

Finally, over at Lover's Lake, the basketball goons find Eddie, who is trying to row a boat to safety. Chief goons Patrick and Jason swim after him, but Vecna suddenly appears and murders Patrick.

## CHAPTER SIX: THE DIVE

We're starting to understand more about Eleven's past thanks to the NINA project, where she remembers that the other kids in her test group didn't trust her. This makes her worried that she might have had something to do with the 1979 explosion that ended their lives. Meanwhile, Mike's group are on their way over to NINA, assisted by Suzie.

In Kamchatka, Hopper and his fellow prisoners are fed a large meal, but he sees through this, knowing full well that this is what happens to people who are about to be sacrificed to the Demogorgon. He steals a cigarette lighter, knowing that the evil beastie is afraid of only one thing: fire. Nearby, Joyce and Murray make Yuri take them to the local town, deciding that Murray will impersonate Yuri in order to get inside the prison. Yes, that does sound a little far-fetched, but bear with us.

Back in Hawkins, stupid Jason is whipping up public outrage against Eddie, who he believes to be leading a demonic cult. More productively, Steve's group find Eddie and Dustin and work out that a new portal to the Upside Down must be at Lover's Lake. Bravely, if also perhaps a little foolishly, Steve dives down to take a look, only to be dragged into the portal, where he is attacked by monstrous bats. Nancy, Robin and Eddie dive in after him...

## CHAPTER SEVEN: THE MASSACRE AT HAWKINS LAB

What the hey? Murray successfully manages to infiltrate the Kamchatka prison, with he, Yuri and Joyce defeating the guards just in time to open the gates and let Hopper and Enzo out. This is just as well, as a minute ago Hopper was fighting the Demogorgon with a burning spear – a battle that was only ever going to end one way.

Back in the US of A, Dustin, Lucas, and Erica figure out that Vecna has created gates to the Upside Down at the places where he murdered someone. This info allows Steve's group to escape the Upside Down in Eddie's trailer, where Chrissy died. Just as they're about to get the heck out, Vecna possesses Nancy, and it's revelation time. She learns

**Above:** Joyce and Murray, clearly regretting their decision to fly on a budget airline this time.

**Right:** Vecna, or Henry Creel as no one calls him, has a gripping backstory, although no one lives long enough to hear it.

that Vecna is in fact Victor Creel's son Henry, a former test subject at the lab where Eleven was raised. Having killed his mother and sister with his powers, Henry was taken by Dr Brenner and became subject '001' in Brenner's attempts to replicate said powers. Later, he became an orderly in Brenner's employ, where he was friendly to Eleven.

Eleven herself now remembers that it was Henry who killed everyone at the lab. She refused to help him carry out the massacre, and he tried to murder her for this: overcoming him, she sent him to the Upside Down, where he gradually transformed into Vecna. Now we get it!

## CHAPTER EIGHT: PAPA

Vecna, in control of Nancy's mind, reveals a diabolical plan for Hawkins: he shows her an image of the town destroyed by cracks in the ground. When he releases her, she discusses this with the rest of the group, who figure that the nasty fellow will need four gates to make this happen. Max plans to lure him into possessing her so that the others can attack him while his attention is on her.

Eleven catches a mental glimpse of this and, realising that she's needed in Hawkins, persuades Owens to send her there. Before this can happen, though, Brenner drugs and traps her, demanding that she completes her training: this leads her to realise that Brenner's agenda over the years has simply been to get her to bring Henry back from the Upside Down.

Sullivan and his soldiers attack the NINA building, doing an efficient job of killing more or less everyone, although Eleven and Brenner escape. Now fully powered up, Eleven